AF352542

THE CATHOLIC UNIVERSITY OF AMERICA
CANON LAW STUDIES
No. 180

Discussions with Non-Catholics

CANONICAL LEGISLATION

BY THE

REV. STEPHEN JOSEPH KELLEHER, A.B., S.T.B., J.C.L.
Priest of the Archdiocese of New York

A DISSERTATION

*Submitted to the Faculty of the School of Canon Law
of the Catholic University of America in Partial
Fulfillment of the Requirements for the Degree of
Doctor of Canon Law*

THE CATHOLIC UNIVERSITY OF AMERICA PRESS
WASHINGTON, D. C.

1943

Nihil Obstat:

CLEMENT V. BASTNAGEL, J.U.D.,
Censor Deputatus.

Washingtonii, D. C., die 6 maii, 1943.

Imprimatur:

✠ FRANCISCUS J. SPELLMAN, D.D.,
Archiepiscopus Neo-Eboracensis.

Neo-Eboraci, die 17 maii, 1943.

COPYRIGHT, 1943

THE CATHOLIC UNIVERSITY OF AMERICA PRESS

Printed by
THE PAULIST PRESS
New York, N. Y.
51

TO
MY FATHER
AND
MOTHER

TABLE OF CONTENTS

CHAPTER III

CHAPTER IV

PART TWO

CONFERENCES

CHAPTER V

CHAPTER VI

PAGE

CHAPTER VII

FOREWORD

IT is a twofold duty of the Catholic Church to safeguard the
unity of faith and of rule which distinguishes her as the true Church
of Christ, and to draw all men within the confines of this unity. The
regulations enacted by the Church concerning the relations of her
subjects with non-Catholics are prompted by the desire to fulfill one,
or both, of these duties. In the ordering of these relations, the
Church must set up defenses lest any of her subjects be lost to the
Catholic unity. At the same time, she must provide for such relations as will draw non-Catholics into the true fold of Christ.

The present study is devoted to a consideration of the ecclesiastical regulations concerning one particular class of these relations,
those, namely, which are entered into when Catholics and non-Catholics, as members of their respective religious bodies, meet for the
sake of discussion. To avoid any misunderstanding, it will be well
to state at the outset that this study is not directly concerned with
the problem of co-operation in worship between Catholics and non-
Catholics. The type of meeting described above may be joined with,
or may result in, co-operation in worship, but, considered in itself,
it prescinds from such co-operation and is confined to discussion.

The very holding of such a discussion necessarily entails cooperation, at least in the wide sense, since it presupposes that the
parties have agreed, at least implicitly, to meet with one another.
If, however, co-operation is understood in the strict sense, as denot-
ing joint or common action on the part of two or more persons for
the purpose of obtaining one and the same end, these discussions
may be divided into two distinct groups insofar as they do, or do not,
involve such co-operation. Discussions which do not involve cooperation in the strict sense are called disputations, that is, oral debates in which the opposing parties, by force of argument and
rhetoric, strive to convince their adversaries and the audience of the
truth of their respective opinions. Discussions in which the participants strive by joint or common action to attain one and the same
end may be called conferences. Unless it is otherwise noted the

word "conference" will be used to denote any discussion other than a disputation, between Catholics and non-Catholics.

In the light of this basic distinction, it has seemed best to treat these two types of discussions separately. The first part of this work, therefore, will be devoted to a consideration of disputations. In the second part, conferences, or discussions between Catholics and non-Catholics other than disputations, will be considered.

The author takes this opportunity to express his sincere gratitude to His Excellency, the Most Reverend Francis Joseph Spellman, Archbishop of New York, for the opportunity afforded him for graduate study. He wishes to acknowledge his indebtedness to the members of the Faculty of the School of Canon Law of the Catholic University for their generous assistance and helpful suggestions in the preparation of this manuscript.

Part I

Disputations

PRELIMINARY NOTIONS

A DISPUTATION may be generically defined as an oral discussion in which opposed opinions are debated or argued. For the sake of clarity and simplicity, disputations will be considered—in the discussion of their nature, divisions, and morality—as having but two opposed opinions and two disputants. The conclusions arrived at, however, will be equally applicable to disputations in which more than two opinions or disputants are involved.

Religious disputations are quite evidently those which concern the truths of faith. In the present treatise only that type of religious disputation will be considered in which of the two opposed opinions under discussion one conforms to Catholic doctrine and the other does not, and in which at least the proponent of the Catholic teaching is a Catholic.

By reason of the listeners present, this type of disputation may be of a public or a merely private character. A disputation is public if it overflows the limits of the private or family circle; this will be determined by all the circumstances, the challenge, the acceptance, the organization, and especially the attendance and the extent to which the meeting becomes known. A private disputation is one which remains within a small circle of a few persons or families, without becoming generally known.[1] The effect of this division upon the morality of disputations will be discussed shortly.

By reason of the ends intended by the Catholic participants, this type of disputation may be material, dubitative, or formal. In a material disputation the champions on both sides are Catholics, and both have the same end in view, namely: the confirmation, clarifica-

---

[1] Bouscaren, "Cooperation with Non-Catholics, Canonical Legislation,"—*Theological Studies*, III (1942), 505.

tion, and explanation of the true Catholic teaching. Material disputations, a common feature in theological schools, do not constitute a canonical problem, and hence they will not be discussed at length. It suffices to say that, due consideration having been given to the provisions of the natural law, they are licit.

A dubitative disputation may be held between a Catholic and a non-Catholic, or between two Catholics. In the former case the Catholic party, not altogether certain in his faith, is seeking to discover which teaching is correct. In the latter case this lack of conviction characterizes at least one of the Catholic parties. It is obviously illicit for a Catholic to participate in such a disputation, for by the very fact that he doubts one of the dogmas of faith he is a heretic.[2] This procedure is contrary to the natural law at all times.

In a formal disputation one of the disputants is a Catholic, the other a non-Catholic. In such a disputation the Catholic champion is firmly convinced of his stand and is earnestly seeking to win approval of his teaching from his adversary and the audience.

Catholic participation in formal disputations is in itself licit and at times even laudable.[3] This fundamental conclusion, however, is but the first step in determining the morality of any particular formal disputation. This determination will ultimately depend upon the circumstances in each particular case.

A Catholic may not licitly participate in a formal disputation unless there exists a well-founded hope that the net results of the disputation will be beneficial to the cause of Christ. In order that this well-founded hope may exist, it is necessary, first of all, that the Catholic champion be firm in his faith and that he be truly capable of defending the doctrines of the Church. Moreover, since even the most eloquent and persuasive of theologians will make little or no impression on a bigoted non-Catholic who is pertinacious in his error, participation in disputations with persons of this kind is ordinarily forbidden to Catholics.

---

[2] Canon 1325, § 2.

[3] St. Thomas Aquinas, *Summa Theologica* (Taurini: Marietti, 1932), IIa IIae, q. X, a. 7, in corp.; Suarez, *Opera Omnia* (ed. nova, a Carolo Berton, 26 vols., Parisiis: apud Ludovicum Vives, 1856-1866), Tom. XII, Tractatus Primus, *De Fide Theologica*, Disp. XX, sec. I.

Even granted, however, that the knowledge and the dispositions of the disputants are all that they should be, in the case of a public disputation no final decision can be made as to the existence of a well-founded hope of resultant good without due consideration of the probable effects of the disputation on the audience. The good results hoped for may be the strengthening of faith in Catholic listeners or the conversion of non-Catholic listeners. Certainly the hope of a good result will be greatly diminished if there is any real danger that the Catholic listeners will be weakened in their faith, scandalized, or unduly shocked by the proceedings. The same is true if there is a probable danger that the non-Catholic listeners will be strengthened in their error.

Thus it may frequently happen that the morality of a formal public disputation will be determined in part or in whole by the anticipated reaction of the audience. For example, participation in a disputation with a bigoted non-Catholic, although ordinarily forbidden, may at times be permitted if there is a probable hope that the disputation will have a good effect upon the audience.

As is evident from these preliminary remarks, the rules governing the morality of formal disputations are found chiefly in the natural law. There has been very little internal evolution in the legislation bearing on this subject. As a result, legislation of a purely ecclesiastical character is reduced to a minimum. There has been an external evolution, an unfolding of the natural law. However, since the guiding principles concerning the morality of these meetings are for the greater part obvious, even the external evolution has been slight. The rôle of the ecclesiastical legislator has been to point out the precepts of the natural law according as they are demanded by historical circumstances, to enact precautionary measures in order that these precepts may be observed (e. g., by requiring the permission of an ecclesiastical superior prior to the holding of a disputation), and to annex punishments to the violation of these precepts and precautionary measures.

In the present treatise ecclesiastical legislation dealing with disputations will be discussed and analyzed. In addition, the outstanding disputations which have taken place since the time of Christ will be briefly considered in order that the significance and development of ecclesiastical legislation may be better understood.

CHAPTER I

FROM THE FIRST CENTURY TO THE TIME OF GRATIAN

ARTICLE 1. OUTSTANDING DISPUTATIONS

THE first account of a disputation between Catholics and non-Catholics after Christ's Ascension is found in the Acts of the Apostles.[1] "But there arose some from the synagogue which is called that of the Freedmen, and of the Cyrenians and of the Alexandrians and of those from Cilicia and the province of Asia, disputing with Stephen." This controversy was evidently provoked by the fact that Stephen was converting some of the Jews to the Christian way of life. The rabbis attempted to argue with him, but "they were not able to withstand the wisdom and the Spirit who spoke." Finally they attempted to put a halt to his good works by misrepresenting his words. Although five groups of Jews are mentioned in the text, it is not certain whether Stephen disputed one, two, or five times. The text is not concerned with this point.[2]

St. Paul engaged in a number of controversies. Just a few of the more important ones will be considered. At Jerusalem, shortly after his conversion, Paul engaged in a debate with the Hellenistic Jews.[3] These Jews composed one of the groups with whom Stephen had disputed.[4] During his second missionary journey, while awaiting Silas and Timothy at Athens, Paul engaged in a dispute with some Epicurean and Stoic philosophers.[5] After this discussion Paul received several converts into the Church. From Athens Paul went on to Corinth. There he taught in the synagogue, laying special emphasis on the fact that Jesus was the Christ.[6] The rabbis contra-

---

[1] VI, 9-11.

[2] Knabenbauer, *Commentarius in Actus Apostolorum* (Parisiis, 1899), pp. 116-117.

[3] Acts VI, 29.

[4] Knabenbauer, *op. cit.*, p. 173.

[5] Acts XVII, 18-34.

[6] Acts XVIII, 1-6.

dicted him, and blasphemed, whereupon he left them and went forth to preach to the Gentiles. At Ephesus Paul's experience was very much the same as at Corinth.[7]

There is no extant account of any religious controversy akin to a prearranged formal disputation earlier than the year 150. About this time a memorable debate took place in Ephesus between St. Justin Martyr and one Trypho, a Jew. This debate was set down in writing by St. Justin, and has come down to us as his *Dialogus Cum Tryphone Judaeo.*[8] It is quite possible that in the written work some details have been added and the form has been changed, but still the work in its foundations seems to reproduce a real colloquy. There are positive indications of this fact in the work itself,[9] and in the writings of St. Jerome (340?-420)[10] and of Eusebius (264?-349?).[11]

The principal topics discussed were the following: the prejudices of the Jews in regard to the Law of Moses and the Christian religion; the scriptural proofs for the Divinity of Christ, His Incarnation, and the Redemption; the biblical prophecies concerning the universality of the Church and the calling of the Gentiles. Although Trypho was not immediately converted as a result of these talks, he was very favorably impressed by the Catholic doctrines and was anxious to know more about them. He and St. Justin parted on the best of terms.[12]

Toward the end of the fourth century a series of prearranged formal disputations began between the Donatists and the Catholic bishops of Africa, particularly St. Augustine (354-430), the Bishop of Hippo. The Donatists, in addition to being schismatics, also upheld the heretical notions that the validity of the sacraments de-

---

[7] Acts XIX, 8-9.

[8] Migne, *Patrologiae Cursus Completus, Series Graeca* (161 vols., Parisiis, 1856-1866), VI, 471-800. Hereafter this work will be cited as *MPG*. Cf. Maran, *Praefatio ad Opera St. Justini—MPG*, VI, 144-151.

[9] *MPG*, VI, 665.

[10] *De Viris Illustribus*, lib. 23—Migne, *Patrologiae Cursus Completus, Series Latina* (221 vols., Parisiis, 1844-1864), XXIII, 641. Hereafter this work will be cited as *MPL*.

[11] *Historia Ecclesiastica*, lib. IV, cap. XVIII—*MPG*, XX, 376.

[12] *MPG*, VI, 800.

pended on the faith and moral purity of the minister, and that sinners were excluded from the body of the Church.

In 377 or 378 St. Augustine held a conference with Fortunius, the Donatist Bishop of Tubursicum.[13] In 398 he entered into an epistolary disputation with Honorat.[14] In 399 he wished to dispute with Crispinus, the Donatist Bishop of Colonia, but the latter refused.[15]

On August 25, 403, the bishops of the VII Council of Carthage, through the mediation of the civil magistrates, invited the Donatists to participate in a formal disputation.[16] The Donatists refused. The invitation was extended once more by the X Council of Carthage on August 23, 405, but to no avail. Finally on October 14, 410, the Emperor Honorius published an edict ordering that a conference be held between the Catholic and the Donatist bishops. Following the publication of this edict a series of formal disputations was held in Carthage on the first, third, and eighth days of June in the year 411. Two hundred eighty-six Catholic bishops and two hundred seventy-nine Donatist bishops were present. The imperial commissioner, Marcellinus, presided. On the first and second days very little was accomplished, but on the third day St. Augustine gained a resounding victory for the Catholics. In his *Breviculus Collationis cum Donatistis* the saint gives us an abridged account of the conferences.[17]

Augustine's last disputation was with Emeritus, the Bishop of Caesarea, in 419. Emeritus had been one of the Donatist champions at Carthage.[18]

St. Augustine was heartily in favor of the disputations with the Donatists, and in this case, certainly, the disputations seem to have accomplished a great deal of good. St. Augustine makes no mention of ecclesiastical legislation in regard to formal disputations. In fact, by his silence he seems to deny that the imperial legislation con-

---

[13] *Epistola XLIV—MPL*, XXXIII, 173-180.

[14] *Epistola XLIX—MPL*, XXXIII, 189-191.

[15] *Epistola LI—MPL*, XXXIII, 191-194.

[16] Mansi, *Sacrorum Conciliorum Nova et Amplissima Collectio* (53 vols. in 60, Parisiis, 1901-1927), III, 787. Hereafter this work will be cited as Mansi.

[17] *MPL*, XLIII, 613-650. ·

[18] *MPL*, XLIII, 689-706.

tained in the Theodosian Code [19] had any effect in this matter. Moreover, in 404, the bishops of the IX Council of Carthage had asked that the imperial laws regarding heretical disturbances be applied to the Donatists.[20] Certainly, if these same laws forbade all formal disputations, some mention would have been made of this fact.

ARTICLE 2. LEGISLATION

In the Theodosian Code one entire title is devoted to a treatment *de his qui super religione contendunt.*[21] Two laws in this title refer to disputations. The first of these [22] forbade public religious controversies under pain of punishment. The punishment is not specified. This law was originally promulgated by Theodosius the Great on June 6, 388.[23] Evidently this law did not have the desired effect in Egypt, for on July 18, 392, Theodosius promulgated another law for this country.[24] This latter legislation was directed against those who continued to cause religious disturbances despite the fact that they had been sentenced for violating the general law. The general law referred to is either the one mentioned above or a law found in the title *De Haereticis.*[25] The violators of the law promulgated for Egypt were to be deported.

[19] Cf. Article 2 of this chapter.

[20] Mansi, III, 794, 1159.

[21] *Codex Theodosianus* (ed. P. Krueger, Th. Mommsen, P. M. Meyer, 3 vols., Berolini, 1905), (16.4).

[22] "Nulli egresso ad publicum vel disceptandi de religione vel tractandi vel consilii aliquid deferendi patescat occasio. Et si quis posthac ausu gravi atque damnabili contra huiusmodi legem veniendum esse crediderit vel insistere motu pestiferae perseverationis audebit, competenti poena et digno supplicio coerceatur."—C. Th. (16.4) 2.

[23] This date is given with the text of the law in the edition of the *Codex Theodosianus* previously cited.

[24] "Deportatione dignus est, qui nec generali lege admonitus nec competenti sententia emendatus et fidem Catholicam turbat et populum."—C. Th. (16.4) 3.

[25] "Ii, qui scaevi dogmatis retinent principatum, hoc est episcopi presbyteri diacones atque lectores et si qui clericatus velamine religioni maculam conantur infligere, sub cuiuslibet haeresis sive erroris nomine constituti ex funestis conciliabulis, seu intra urbem seu in surburbanis esse videantur, omni modo propellantur."—C. Th. (16.5) 19.

By means of these laws Theodosius hoped to put an end to heretical disturbances in the East, so that there would be peace on the home front while he took up his campaign against Maximus the Tyrant.[26] These laws were passed, therefore, to put an end to the religious controversies which were disturbing the peace of the Empire. Formal disputations were not forbidden in themselves, but only insofar as they disturbed the public order. Thus it is understandable why the legislation of Theodosius the Great is not mentioned during the conferences of St. Augustine with the Donatists. One of the ends of these laws, at least from the point of view of the Emperor, was the safeguarding of the public order and the civil peace.

In the year 451, at the time of the Council of Chalcedon, the Emperors Valentinian III (425-455) and Marcian (450-457) issued an edict designed to prevent any contentious discussions concerning the decrees approved at the Council. According to this edict the decrees of the Council were to be considered the last word in matters of faith. Any disputation or contradictory discussion concerning them was a sin to be punished not only by the judgment of God, but also by the laws of the Empire.[27] Pope St. Leo I (440-461),

---

[26] Gothofredus, *Codex Theodosianus cum Perpetuis Commentariis* (6 vols. in 7, Lipsiae, 1743), lib. XVI, tit. IV, *De his qui super religione contendunt.*

[27] "Tandem aliquando, quod summis votis atque studiis optabamus, evenit. Remota est de orthodoxa Christianorum lege contentio, tandem remedia culpabilis erroris inventa sunt, et discors populorum sententia in unum consensum concordiamque convenit. E diversis enim provinciis religiossimi sacerdotes Chalcedonem venerunt juxta nostra praecepta, et quid observari in religione debeat, perspicua definitione docuerunt. Cesset igitur jam profana contentio. Nam vere impius et sacrilegus est, qui post tot sacerdotum sententiam, opinioni suae aliquid tractandum relinquit. Extremae quippe dementiae est, in medio et perspicuo die commentitium lumen inquirere. Quisquis enim post veritatem repertam aliquid ulterius discutit, mendacium quaerit. . . . Constat enim, hinc haereticae insaniae exordia fomitemque praeberi, dum publice quidam disputant atque contendunt. Universi ergo quae a sancta synodo Chalcedonensi statuta sunt custodire debebunt, nihil postea dubitari. Hoc itaque nostrae commoniti serenitatis edicto, abstinete a profanis vocibus, et ulterius desinite de divinis disputare: quod nefas est. Quis non solum judicio divino peccatum hoc, prout credimus, punietur, verum etiam legum et judicum auctoritate coercebitur."— Mansi, VII, 475.

if he did not expressly approve the edict itself, heartily endorsed the sentiments expressed in it.[28]

A substantial part of the edict was taken over in the Code of Justinian.[29] This law was directed against dubitative disputations. Only those who denied or doubted the truths of the faith were subject to punishment. The law did not forbid Catholics from entering disputations for the purpose of defending the faith of Chalcedon. Participation in formal disputations, therefore, was not prohibited.

The latter-day authors concur in this conclusion.[30] According to Brunneman (1608-1672), *"hic disputationes eae prohibentur, quae ad Catholicam fidem subvertendam, aut tantum in dubium revocandam moventur, non quae pro stabilienda Christiana religione instituantur."* [31] Barbosa (1589-1649) likewise considers this law as

[28] *"Litteras clementiae tuae,"* 1 dec. 457; *"Multo gaudio mens,"* 21 mart. 458; *"Multis manifestisque,"* 17 aug. 458—Jaffé, *Regesta Pontificum Romanorum ab condita Ecclesia ad annum post Christum natum MCXCVIII,* 2. ed. cura Wattenbach, Loewenfeld, Kaltenbrunner, Ewald (2 vols. in 1, Lipsiae, 1885-1888), nn. 532, 539, 541. Hereafter this work will be cited as J. L., J. K. or J. E., to denote the editors of this edition of Jaffé's work.

[29] "Nemo clericus vel militans vel alterius cuiuslibet condicionis de fide Christiana publice turbis coadunatis et audientibus tractare conetur in posterum, ex hoc tumultus et perfidiae occasionem requirens. Nam iniuriam facit iudicio reverendissimae synodi, si quis semel iudicata ac recte disposita revolvere et publice disputare contendit, cum ea, quae nunc de Christiana fide a sacerdotibus qui Chalcedone convenerunt, per nostra praecepta statuta sunt, iuxta apostolicas expositiones et statuta sanctorum patrum trecentorum decem et octo et centum quinquaginta definita esse noscuntur. Nam in contemptores huius legis poena non deerit, quia non solum contra fidem vere expositam veniunt, sed etiam iudaeis et paganis ex huiusmodi certamine profanant veneranda mysteria. Igitur si clericus erit, qui publice tractare de religione ausus fuerit, consortio clericorum removebitur; si vero militia praeditus sit, cingulo spoliabitur; ceteri etiam huiusmodi rei criminis, si quidem liberi sint, de hac sacratissima urbe pellentur, pro vigore iudiciario etiam competentibus suppliciis subiugandi, sin vero servi, severissimis animadversionibus plectentur."—*Codex Iustinianus* (recognovit et retractavit P. Krueger, Berolini: apud Weidmannos, 1928-1929), C. (1.1) 4.

[30] Although this chapter deals only with the legislation promulgated up to the time of Gratian, nevertheless the opinions of the post-Reformation authors must be considered, for these laws were still considered as being in force at that time.

[31] *Commentarius in Codicem Justinianeum* (2 vols., Coloniae Allobrogum, 1771), lib. I, tit. I, 1. *Nemo,* 4, n. 2.

forbidding only dubitative disputations.[32] Gonzalez-Tellez (+1649), while he does not treat Roman Law *ex professo*, remarks in his commentary on the legislation of the Gregorian decretals that the law of Justinian deals only with dubitative disputations.[33]

This is also the conclusion of Reiffenstuel (1641-1703),[34] Ferraris (+ c. 1760),[35] Petra (1662-1747)[36] and Pignatelli (c. 1600-1675).[37]

Several of the latter-day canonical commentators[38] interpret the Justinian law as forbidding formal disputations. However, when one considers the text, the context, and the circumstances under which the law was passed, this conclusion scarcely seems tenable.

In the year 492, in a letter to Faustus, the papal legate at Constantinople, Pope Gelasius I (492-496) wrote as follows: *"Canonum magistris, atque custodibus, nobis nullum fas est inire certamen cum hominibus communionis alienae."*[39] The pontiff did not wish his legate to have any discussions or disputations with pertinacious heretics in matters of faith.

---

[32] *Collectanea ex doctoribus tum priscis, tum neotericis in Codicem Justiniani* (2 vols., Lugduni, 1657), lib. I, tit. I, 1. III, nn. 1-2.

[33] *Commentaria Perpetua in Singulos Textus Quinque Librorum Decretalium Gregorii IX* (5 vols. in 4, Venetiis, 1699), lib. V, tit. VII, cap. XII, n. 9. Hereafter this work will be cited by the name of the author.

[34] *Jus Canonicum Universum* (5 vols. in 7, Parisiis, 1864-1870), lib. V, tit. VII, n. 29. Hereafter this work will be cited by the name of the author.

[35] *Bibliotheca Canonica, Juridica, Moralis, Theologica, nec non Ascetica, Polemica, Rubricistica, Historica* (9 vols., Romae, 1885-1899), "Fides," n. 38. Hereafter this work will be cited by the name of the author.

[36] *Commentaria ad Constitutiones Apostolicas* (5 vols. in 2, Venetiis, 1729), Constitutio II Nicolai III, incipiens Noverit, n. 18. Hereafter merely the number will be cited when reference is made to this work of Petra, and the work will be cited as *Commentaria*.

[37] *Novissimae Consultationes Canonicae* (2 vols. in 1, Cosmopoli, 1711), tomus prior, consultatio XLV. Hereafter this work will be cited as *Consultationes*.

[38] E. g., Farinacius, *Variarum Quaestionum et Communium Opinionum Criminalium* (Romae, 1616), *Liber V. de haeresi*, tit. 18, quaest. 178, n. 108; Pirhing, *Jus Canonicum Nova Methodo Explicatum* (5 vols. in 4, Dilingae, 1674-1678), lib. V, tit. VII, n. 27. Hereafter these works will be cited by the names of the authors.

[39] *"Ego quoque mente,"* 1 nov. 493—J. L., n. 622.

These very same words were incorporated into the *Decretum Gratiani* [40] and as such they have been subject to a variety of interpretation. Joannes Teutonicus (+1245), in a *glossa* attached to the text of the law, points out that disputations are licit if they are held for the purpose of convincing heretics of their errors. He adds that such disputations are illicit if the Catholic party is in doubt concerning his faith. [41] The conclusion from these remarks seems to be that the law forbade only dubitative disputations. That this is the conclusion of the glossator seems certain because the parallel texts which he cites from Justinian Law [42] and the Gregorian Decretals [43] can refer only to this type of disputation. Reiffenstuel [44] states that this conclusion is the common opinion confirmed by the universal practice of the Church. He says that the arguments for this conclusion are drawn from the *glossa* and the context of the law.

Schmalzgrueber (1663-1735) [45] and Pirhing (1606-1679) [46] interpret the law as forbidding formal disputations, but they qualify this conclusion with conditions which almost render it nil. Unlearned clerics are forbidden to enter into such disputations for obvious reasons. Learned clerics are forbidden to enter into disputations with heretics who are obstinate and pertinacious in their errors. These authors point out that there is very little hope for the conversion of such heretics, and that disputations in such cases will only cause an increase of hostility. Nevertheless, both Schmalzgrueber and Pirhing concede that this law does not forbid learned clerics from disputing, even publicly, with heretics, for the purpose of refuting heretical errors and for the defense of the Catholic faith.

---

[40] C. 36, C. XXIV, q. 3.

[41] "Ergo cum haereticis non est disputandum nec cum aliquo est de fide disputandum. Extra de haere. ca. 1 et nemo. Sed ad hoc potest disputari cum eis, ut convincantur, non ut in dubium revocent fidem nostram, ut extra de haer. c. 1."—*Glossa* ad c. 36, C. XXIV, q. 3, ad v. *Certamen.*

[42] C. (1.1) 4.

[43] C. 1, X, *de haereticis*, V, 7.

[44] Lib. V, tit. VII, n. 29.

[45] *Jus Ecclesiasticum Universum* (5 vols. in 12, Romae, 1843-1845), lib. V, tit. VII, n. 64. Hereafter this work will be cited by the name of the author.

[46] Lib. V, tit. VII, n. 27.

Thus in the last analysis they seem to agree with the author of the *glossa*.

Although they do not expressly consider this law, Gonzalez-Tellez,[47] Ferraris,[48] and Petra,[49] since they admit that clerics may engage in formal disputations, seem to draw implicitly the same conclusion.

The authors thus far considered interpret the words *canonum magistris atque custodibus* as signifying all clerics. Pignatelli[50] introduces a new note. He restricts the meaning of the words to clerics in authority, that is, to the pope, to those present at ecclesiastical councils, to bishops, and to the judges of the inquisition. He reasons that it is below the dignity of these ecclesiastical persons to enter into disputations with heretics, for it would then appear that heretics are on an equal footing with those in authority. He points out that Pope Gelasius, in first promulgating this legislation, was forbidding that heretics be admitted into ecclesiastical councils on a par with those in authority. His conclusion, therefore, is that formal disputations, except in urgent cases, are forbidden to those in authority. This restrictive interpretation of the law is apparently well-reasoned, but it finds no support among the other authors. According to the common interpretation these words are rather a warning to all clerics that they should abstain from discussing religion with heretics who are obstinate and pertinacious in their errors. No matter which interpretation is accepted, one conclusion is certain: the words of Pope Gelasius do not create a purely ecclesiastical law. In both interpretations they simply corroborate principles which flow from the Divine constitution of the Church.

During the first twelve centuries of her existence, therefore, the Church did not deem it necessary to curtail formal disputations by means of purely ecclesiastical prohibitions or penalties. As is evidenced by the work of St. Stephen, St. Paul, St. Justin Martyr and St. Augustine, she accepted the fact that under favorable conditions formal disputations could be an apt means of safeguarding and extending the true faith.

[47] Lib. V, tit. VII, cap. XII, n. 9.
[48] "Fides," n. 38.
[49] *Commentaria*, n. 18.
[50] *Consultationes*, t. I, c. XLV.

CHAPTER II

FROM THE END OF THE TWELFTH CENTURY TO THE *LIBER SEXTUS*

ARTICLE 1. OUTSTANDING DISPUTATIONS

DURING the twelfth and thirteenth centuries a group of heresies arose which were to cause considerable trouble before they were finally extirpated by the ecclesiastical authorities. The Waldensians and the Albigenses, two of the more formidable of these new heretical sects, will be considered insofar as they were the occasions of several noteworthy disputations.

The Waldensians, founded by Peter Waldo in Lyons about the year 1176, were originally a kind of penitential brotherhood of the laity vowed to practice poverty and to preach it. At first their only fault lay in their refusal to refrain from preaching without the permission of the ecclesiastical authorities. From this comparatively minor error, however, they fell into the pitfall of anti-clericalism, and finally into the abyss of heresy.[1]

There is extant at least one account of a disputation between the Waldensians and the Catholics. This debate took place in the diocese of Narbonne, in the year 1190, at the request of the archbishop, and therefore with his approval. These details are given, as is also a glowing account of the Catholic victory in the disputation, by one Bernard, in his *Adversus Waldensium Sectam Liber*. Bernard was a Praemonstratensian monk, the abbot of the monastery at Foncaude.[2]

The idealism of Peter Waldo found no place in the minds of the original Albigenses,[3] who were rather enthusiastic pioneers of a new

---

[1] Hughes, *A History of the Church* (2 vols., New York: Sheed & Ward, 1935), II, 375-376. Hereafter this work will be cited by the name of the author.

[2] *MPL*, CCIV, 793.

[3] From the fact that Albi in southern France was one of the strongholds of the movement, the Cathars of the twelfth and thirteenth centuries are commonly called Albigenses.

anti-Christian social order. These heretics were the heirs of the immoral Manichaean doctrines which had once enslaved St. Augustine.[4]

At the end of the twelfth century Languedoc in southern France was one of the Albigensian strongholds. In 1204 Innocent III (1198-1216) had appointed an abbot and two monks of the Cistercian order as apostolic legates to combat the heresy in this section.[5] These good monks went to work with a will, but in spite of their efforts the heretics continued to gain ground. This temporary failure and the ensuing disappointment of the legates is witnessed in another letter of Innocent III in 1205.[6]

The legates were at a loss as to how to proceed when they had the good fortune to meet Diego, the Bishop of Osma in Spain, who had recently visited Rome, and was passing through France on the way to his own diocese. Among his companions was a young man named Dominic. In an attempt to aid the legates, Diego made the simple but saintly suggestion that they put aside all signs of worldly riches, and carry on their work in the spirit of evangelical poverty. Thus traveling by foot without gold or silver, and proceeding in humility, they would effect conversions by preaching and example. Diego himself inaugurated this movement. He sent his companions home, with the exception of Dominic, and joined forces with the legates.[7]

Together they set out on their mission. In addition to preaching, they entered into a number of disputations with the heretics. During the years 1206-1207 they disputed at Beziers, Carcassone, Montreal, Pamiers and other cities in southern France. They were successful in refuting the heretics, but the final result was often

---

[4] Hughes, II, 380.

[5] Ep. *"Etsi navicula nostra,"* 31 maii 1204—*Regesta Pontificum Romanorum inde ab anno post Christum natum MCXCVIII ad annum MCCCIV* (2 vols., edidit Augustus Potthast: Berolini, 1874-1875), n. 2229. Hereafter this work will be cited as Potthast.

[6] *"Debitum caritatis,"* 26 ian. 1205—Potthast, n. 2391.

[7] *Petri Vallium Sarnaii Monachi Hystoria Albigensis* (publiée pour la Société de l'histoire de France par Pascal Guébin et Ernest Lyon, 2 tomes, Paris: Librairie Ancienne Honoré Champion, 1926), I, nn. 20-21. Hereafter this work will be cited as Petrus Sarnensis (+1218), *Hystoria Albigensis.*

further alienation rather than conversion.[8] The murder of one of the legates, and the war which followed, put an end to this crusade of preaching.

There does not seem to be any explicit papal approval of the disputations, but since Innocent III continued to encourage the legates,[9] and the number of Catholic participants increased,[10] it can be concluded that the disputations were accepted as a good and useful means of refuting the heretics and of defending the Catholic faith. Moreover, the performance of a number of miracles was a sign of divine approbation.[11] Finally, the character of the persons involved leads one to believe that they were acting well within the law.

The Albigenses ceased to be a menace by the end of the thirteenth century, but until that time the Church found it necessary to use strong penal measures against the heretics. Evidence of this is found in the legislation of the Council of Narbonne in 1235,[12] and in a bull of Innocent IV, *"Ad extirpanda de."* [18]

Article 2. The Law of the Liber Sextus

In addition to the dissension caused by numerous heresies, the Church of the late middle ages was also disturbed by the growth of laicism and anticlericalism. This is evidenced in the history of the Waldensians, who felt that it was their duty to preach the gospel even though they were not clerics. One of the means used to crush these erroneous notions was a law forbidding lay people to participate in formal disputations. This law, which was promulgated by several popes and eventually found its way into the *Liber Sextus*, retained its original wording throughout its history.

The text of the law reads:

> Inhibemus quoque, ne cuiquam laicae personae liceat publice vel privatim de fide Catholica disputare. Qui vero contra fecerit, excommunicationis laqueo innodetur.

[8] Petrus Sarnensis, *Hystoria Albigensis*, I, nn. 22-48.

[9] Ep. *"Excursus saeculi tendentis,"* 17 nov. 1206—Potthast, n. 2912.

[10] Petrus Sarnensis, *Hystoria Albigensis*, I, n. 47.

[11] Petrus Sarnensis, *Hystoria Albigensis*, I, nn. 25, 54.

[12] Mansi, XXIII, 356-366.

[18] 15 maii 1252—Potthast, n. 14592. Cf. n. 14603.

This law is found for the first time in a constitution of Gregory IX promulgated in the year 1235.[14] It appears again in constitutions of Innocent IV,[15] Alexander IV [16] and Nicholas IV.[17] Finally, as contained in the constitution of Alexander IV, it was embodied in the *Liber Sextus* [18] on the third of March, 1298, and as such it was in force until the advent of the Code in 1918.

At first sight the law seems to be very clear, but a glance at the commentators will serve to dispel that notion. What type of disputation is forbidden? What persons are subject to the law? Granted that the punishment is a *ferendae sententiae* penalty, is there required another *monitio* besides that given in the law? These are some of the questions which must be answered before the law can be fully understood.

The authors [19] are generally agreed that the law does not forbid material disputations.[20] Petra (1662-1747)[21] and Delbene (1623-1673)[22] point out that, since the law is directed only against the participation of lay people in disputations, it cannot be said to include dubitative disputations, for these are also forbidden to clerics by the natural law. The law, therefore, is directed against formal disputations, wherein a Catholic party, firm in his faith, is trying to

[14] *"Excommunicamus et anathematizamus,"* 9 nov. 1235—Potthast, n. 10043.

[15] *"Noverit universitas vestra,"* 15 iun. 1254—Potthast, n. 15425.

[16] *"Quicumque haereticos credentes."* This constitution was promulgated during the reign of Alexander IV (December 12, 1254—May 15, 1261). The exact date is not known.—Potthast, n. 18115.

[17] *"Noverit universitas vestra,"* 3 mart. 1291—Potthast, n. 23589. In the *Bullarium Romanum* (24 vols. et Appendix, Augustae Taurinorum, 1857-1872), IV, 47, this constitution is falsely ascribed to Nicholas III under date of March 3, 1280. Cf. Potthast, nn. 21689, 23589.

[18] C. 2, *de haereticis*, V, 2, in VI°.

[19] Schmalzgrueber, lib. V, tit. VII, n. 66; Gonzalez-Tellez, lib. V, tit. VII, cap. XII, n. 8; Pignatelli, *Consultationes*, t. I, c. XLV.

[20] The authors of the post-Reformation period are considered at length inasmuch as this law was in force until the advent of the Code. Moreover, with the growth of the Protestant sects, the law took on a new importance.

[21] *Commentaria*, n. 18.

[22] *De Officio S. Inquisitionis* (2 vols., Lugduni, 1666), dubitatio CLIV, petitio VI, n. 8. All future references to Delbene will be from this same *dubitatio* and *petitio*; hence only the number will be cited.

convince a non-Catholic of his error, or at least is defending the faith.[23]

The chief point of discussion is in regard to the meaning of the words *laicae personae*. In the *Glossa Ordinaria* of Ioannes Andreae (1270-1348)[24] it is noted that in some places at the time of the promulgation of the law the word *laici* was used to signify the ignorant or the unlearned, and the word *clerici* to signify the learned or educated. Therefore, one who understood the words of the legislator in this sense would say that the law affected all and only unlearned persons, whether they were lay people or clerics in the ordinary sense of the terms. However, the author of the *Glossa*, having made the distinction, discards it, and accepts the words in their ordinary sense.[25] This unusual distinction was accepted by only a few authors.[26].

Dandinus (early 18th century) contends that the law affects only unlearned lay people.[27] He denies that the power of orders has anything to do with the power to dispute, and says that disputations are forbidden to lay people only because as a rule they are not sufficiently instructed in matters of faith. He goes on to say that learned lay people are not forbidden to dispute, because if the end of the law ceases, the law itself ceases.

---

[23] Ferraris, "Fides," n. 38; Barbosa, *Collectanea doctorum tam veterum quam recentiorum in jus pontificium universum* (6 vols. in 3, Lugduni, 1716), lib. V, tit. II, cap. II in VI°, n. 16; Gonzalez-Tellez, lib. V, tit. VII, cap. XII, n. 8. Hereafter the work of Barbosa will be cited simply by the name of the author.

[24] "Forte intellexerunt de laico ad modum ultramontanorum, qui illiteratos laicos vocant, et litteratos clericos vocant. Quid enim est dicere quod ruralis clericus disputando de fide non incidat in hanc poenam et doctor decretorum incidat? Tamen sufficit ita esse scriptum, et solum duo sunt Christianorum genera, clerici et laici."—*Glossa* ad c. 2, *de haereticis*, V, 2, in VI°, ad v. *laicae.*

[25] Here it may be noted that Ioannes Andreae was a layman, a *doctor decretorum*, and probably took this opportunity to show that he did not approve of the law as it was written.

[26] Cf. Ferraris, "Fides," n. 37, nota 2; Patuzzi, *De Praeceptis Fidei et de Vitiis Fidei Oppositis*, cap. IV, 3—*Theologiae Cursus Completus* (28 vols., edidit J. P. Migne, Parisiis, 1858-1860), VI, 630-631.

[27] *De Suspectis de Haeresi* (Romae, 1703), pars prima, cap. V, sect. II, nn. 101-102.

However, most of the authors are agreed that this law affected all lay people, including the learned,[28] but did not affect even unlearned clerics. Certainly this interpretation seems more correct in the light of the events which were taking place at the time the law was passed.[29] Pignatelli[30] and Delbene[31] add that religious were not bound by this law because they have the privileges of clerics.

The reasons given in favor of this opinion are: first, *"Ubi lex non distinguit, nec nos distinguere debemus;"*[32] second, *"Leges latae ad praecavendum periculum generale, urgent, etiamsi in casu particulari periculum non adsit;"*[33] third, the right to enter disputations is reserved to clerics by reason of their office.[34] This last reason is based on the laws which forbid lay people to teach and to preach.[35] The reasons given for the promulgation of the laws are: first, lay people are not sufficiently instructed in matters of faith;[36] second, the danger of perversion must be avoided;[37] third, such an office should be reserved to ecclesiastical persons;[38] fourth, there is danger that heretics may be confirmed in their errors.[39]

The proponents of this last and common opinion, according to which all and only lay people were forbidden to take part in formal disputations, admit that in certain circumstances a learned lay per-

---

[28] Ferraris, "Fides," n. 39; Schmalzgrueber, lib. V, tit. VII, n. 64; Pignatelli, *Consultationes*, t. I, c. XLV; Reiffenstuel, lib. V, tit. VII, n. 27; Gonzalez-Tellez, lib. V, tit. VII, cap. XII, n. 9; Petra, *Commentaria*, n. 22; Delbene, *De Officio S. Inquisitionis*, n. 8.

[29] Schmalzgrueber, lib. V, tit. VII, n. 65; Pirhing, lib. V, tit. VII, n. 27; Barbosa, lib. V, tit. II, cap. II, in VI°, n. 15; Petra, *Commentaria*, n. 22.

[30] *Consultationes*, t. I, c. XLV.

[31] *De Officio S. Inquisitionis*, n. 6.

[32] Reiffenstuel, lib. V, tit. VII, n. 27; Schmalzgrueber, lib. V, tit. VII, n. 64.

[33] Schmalzgrueber, lib. V, tit. VII, n. 64.

[34] Gonzalez-Tellez, lib. V, tit. VII, cap. XII, n. 9; Pignatelli, *Consultationes*, t. I, c. XLV; Delbene, *De Officio S. Inquisitionis*, n. 10.

[35] E. g., "Mulier, quamvis docta et sancta, viros in conventu docere non praesumat. Laicus autem praesentibus clericis (nisi ipsis rogantibus) docere non audeat."—C. 29, D. 23.

[36] Reiffenstuel, lib. V, tit. VII, n. 26; Gonzalez-Tellez, lib. V, tit. VII, cap. XII, n. 9.

[37] Reiffenstuel, lib. V, tit. VII, n. 26; Schmalzgrueber, lib. V, tit. VII, n. 64.

[38] C. 29, D. 23.

[39] Reiffenstuel, lib. V, tit. VII, n. 26.

son would not be bound by the law. For example, a person who had the permission of a legitimate ecclesiastical authority to enter into a disputation would not be subject to the punishment of excommunication since such permission would be equivalent to a dispensation.[40] Then, too, in the case wherein a non-Catholic was disturbing the faith of the people, and no worthy cleric was present to refute him, a learned lay person would be bound in charity to defend the faith.[41]

Finally, some authors maintain that in Germany and in other places where heretics were numerous, learned lay people did not incur the excommunication if they disputed with heretics. They say that in such places the law was either never received in use or that if it had been received it was abrogated by contrary custom.[42] The reasons given for the cessation of the law in certain places are scarcely in accordance with fundamental legal principles. If the law did really cease under given circumstances, this could only be due to the explicit or implicit revocation of the legislator.

All the authors are agreed that the punishment of excommunication was a *ferendae sententiae* penalty because of the use of the subjunctive *innodetur*,[43] but there are some [44] who maintain that the warning in the law was not sufficient. They say that the excommunication was not incurred except by one who, after a warning other than that contained in the law, continued contumaciously to transgress it.

The law of the *Liber Sextus* has been considered at length because of the new element contained in it. Lay people, even though they might be capable and worthy of disputing, were forbidden to

---

[40] Pignatelli, *Consultationes*, t. I, c. XLV.

[41] Ferraris, "Fides," n. 40; Schmalzgrueber, lib. V, tit. VII, n. 66; Barbosa, lib. V, tit. II, cap. II, in VI°, n. 17.

[42] Reiffenstuel, lib. V, tit. VII, n. 28; Ferraris, "Fides," n. 40 ("Haereticus," n. 27); Schmalzgrueber, lib. V, tit. VII, n. 68; Pignatelli, *Consultationes*, t. I, c. XLV.

[43] Ioannes Andreae, *Glossa*, ad c. 2 *de haereticis*, V, 2, in VI°, ad v. *innodetur;* Gonzalez-Tellez, lib. V, tit. VII, cap. XII, n. 9; Pirhing, lib. V, tit. VII, n. 28; Reiffenstuel, lib. V, tit. VII, n. 2.

[44] Barbosa, lib. V, tit. II, cap. II, in VI°, n. 18; Delbene, *De Officio S. Inquisitionis*, n. 22.

do so unless they had the permission of their ecclesiastical superiors. Anyone guilty of disobeying the law was liable to the punishment of excommunication.

Then, too, this law of the *Liber Sextus* is especially noteworthy because it contains the first purely ecclesiastical legislation on disputations. The law is purely ecclesiastical insofar as it forbids lay people to participate in private formal disputations and threatens with the punishment of excommunication those lay people who participate in formal disputations, whether private or public, without permission. As will be seen in Chapter IV, the prohibition against lay people participating in public formal disputations is not a purely ecclesiastical measure, but a necessary consequence flowing from the public law of the Church.

Since the general policy of the Church after the Reformation was to forbid both the laity and the clergy from participating in formal disputations, it seems strange that the authors of the seventeenth and eighteenth centuries should devote so much energy to the interpretation of this law which affected only lay people. More than likely they did so in view of the heavy penalty annexed to the law. Even after the Reformation no express punishment was enacted for clerics who took part in formal disputations without permission.

CHAPTER III

FROM THE PROTESTANT REVOLT TO THE CODE

Article 1. Outstanding Disputations

For one hundred and fifty years after Luther posted his theses concerning indulgences on the doors of the Augustinian monastery church at Wittenberg, disputations and formal attempts at reunion were a common occurrence. It was during this period that the Church learned by bitter experience that disputations and doctrinal conferences rarely resulted in any lasting good. This fact is witnessed by the attitude of the Church toward these meetings from the seventeenth century to the present day.

The first disputation of note during this period was held at Leipzig from June 27 to July 15, 1519. John Eck (c. 1486-1543), the most powerful defender of the papacy against the Reformers in Germany, debated with Luther (1483-1546) and Karlstadt (c. 1480-1541). Eck triumphed in this disputation insofar as he showed Luther to be a heretic who wished to overthrow the authority of the councils and the Church.[1] Luther, however, although soundly beaten, gained the solid advantage of receiving publicity for his cause and of seeing attached to it a heightened importance in the estimation of the populace.[2] This meeting, as so many of the later ones, only served to alienate the parties involved.

The Catholic theologians, led by Eck, appeared to have entered this disputation without any sign of approval or disapproval from the higher Church authorities. After the disputation there is no sign of an official reprimand. Rather, it seems that Eck's plan of action was implicitly approved inasmuch as he was summoned to Rome, shortly afterwards, by Leo X (1513-1521) to report on con-

---

[1] Grisar, *Martin Luther, His Life and Work* (adapted from the second German edition by Frank J. Eble, edited by Arthur Preuss, St. Louis: B. Herder, 1930), p. 116. Hereafter this work will be cited by the name of the author.

[2] Alzog, *Manual of Universal Church History* (translated, with additions, from the ninth and last German edition by F. J. Pabisch and Thos. S. Byrne, 3 vols., Cincinnati: Robert Clarke & Co., 1878), III, 24. Hereafter this work will be cited by the name of the author.

ditions in Germany. At other meetings the granting of papal permission, if not also of approbation, is evident, as for example at the Hagenau-Worms-Ratisbon Conferences (June 1540-June 1541) when Cardinal Gasparo Contarini (1483-1542) was present as the papal legate.[3] On at least a few occasions high ecclesiastical dignitaries played prominent rôles in disputations. In 1561 the Cardinal of Lorraine (1524-1574) was a participant in a disputation at Poissy.[4] In 1645 Ladislaus IV, King of Poland (1632-1648), and Lubienski, the Archbishop of Gnesen and the Primate of Poland (1641-1652), fostered a series of disputations at Thorn.[5]

Despite the fact that most of the disputations which took place after the Protestant Revolt injured rather than aided the Catholic cause, at least one Catholic champion made good use of this form of preaching. St. Francis de Sales (1567-1622), before he became the Bishop of Geneva (1602-1622), was the leading figure in a number of disputations in Switzerland. In at least one meeting he converted a Calvinist minister, and on numerous other occasions, to the dismay and discomfiture of his opponents, he won over the audience completely. His reputation for piety and learning was so well respected that at times the heretics refused to dispute with him.[6]

The success of St. Francis, however, was exceptional. As a general rule, with each succeeding attempt at reunion it became more apparent that reconciliation was impossible.[7] Frequently, as at Nüremberg and Augsburg,[8] the lay rulers dominated the scene. Then, too, there were other dangers involved. Catholics were so desirous of reunion that they went too far in making concessions. Moreover, these disputations tended to discredit the Catholic cause

---

[3] Grisar, pp. 444-454.

[4] Alzog, III, 273.

[5] Alzog, III, 444-447.

[6] Burton, *The Life of St. Francis de Sales* (adapted from the Abbé Hamon's *Vie de S. Francois de Sales*, 2 vols., London: Burns, Oates & Washbourne, Ltd., 1925), I, 162-165, 168-170, 190-195; Gallizia, *The Life of St. Francis de Sales, Bishop and Prince of Geneva* (translated from the Italian, London, 1854), I, 239, 296, 307.

[7] For a complete list of the more important discussions see H. Quilliet, "Controverses," *Dictionaire de Théologie Catholique*, III, 1694-1748.

[8] Alzog, III, 75-87; Grisar, p. 374.

by giving the impression that points of dogma already defined by the Church could be revised at such joint conferences with heretics. Finally, in nearly every case the disagreement after the disputation was worse than before.[9]

The United States has seen its share of disputations. During the nineteenth century, when the Protestant crusade against the Catholic Church in America was in full swing, oral and written controversies between Catholics and non-Catholics were an established part of the order of the day. Here, however, it was not a question of reunion. Each group was intent upon overpowering the other by force of argument and rhetoric. These dialectic discussions only served to heighten the animosity which already existed between Catholics and non-Catholics. Not infrequently what began as a peaceful meeting ended in a riot. More than likely the Catholic champions felt that participation in these controversies was the only means of combatting the libel and slander which was being heaped against the Catholic Church by all types of Protestants.[10]

[9] Alzog, III, 442, 443, 447.

[10] Billington, *The Protestant Crusade, 1800-1860* (New York: The Macmillan Co., 1938), pp. 32, 58-66, 253-256; Steinbacher-Berg, *Discussion held in Lebanon, Pa., on Mon., Tues., Wed., 17, 18, 19 Oct. 1842, between Nicholas Steinbacher of the Roman Catholic and Joseph Frederick Berg of the Reformed Church* (Philadelphia, 1842); Hughes-Breckinridge, *A Discussion on the Question "Is the Roman Catholic Religion, in any or in all of its Principles or Doctrines, Inimical to Civil or Religious Liberty?" and the Question "Is the Presbyterian Religion, in any or in all of its Principles or Doctrines, Inimical to Civil or Religious Liberty?" By the Rev. John Hughes of the R. C. Church and the Rev. John Breckinridge of the Presbyterian Church* (Baltimore: John Murphy & Co.); Purcell, *The Vickers and Purcell Controversy* (2. ed., Cincinnati: Benziger Bros., 1868).

In England, and even in Ireland, there were some public discussions during the nineteenth century. McGuire-Pope, *Authenticated report of the discussion which took place between the Rev. Richard T. P. Pope and the Rev. Thomas McGuire in the lecture room of the Dublin institution, on the 19, 20, 21, 23, 24, 25, of April 1827* (Dublin: 1827); McGuire-Gregg, *Authenticated Report of the Discussion between the Rev. T. D. Gregg and the Rev. Thomas McGuire* (Dublin: Richard Coyne, 1839); Naghten-Blakeney, *Discussion at Worksop between the Rev. Richard P. Blakeney and the Rev. J. B. Naghten, O.M.I., held in the Music Hall, Worksop, on the evenings of Jan. 30, 31, and Feb. 1, 1850* (reported verbatim by Thomas Whitehead, London, 1850).

ARTICLE 2. LEGISLATION

The law of the *Liber Sextus* was the last general legislation concerning disputations until the promulgation of the Code. However, during the intervening years the mind of the Church was made clear through replies of the Holy Office and of the Sacred Congregation for the Propagation of the Faith.

In a collection of the resolutions and responses of the Holy Office found in the *Analecta Ecclesiastica*[11] it is asserted that permission to participate in disputations with heretics has *always* been denied to Catholics by the Holy Office because these disputations are without value. It is noted, nevertheless, that they have *sometimes* been permitted for the purpose of converting heretics. Since these two statements, if they are accepted as they stand, necessarily involve a contradiction, it must be concluded that the compiler of this collection meant to say that disputations have *generally* been forbidden because they are *usually* without value.[12]

Pignatelli[13] sums up the attitude of the Holy Office in very much the same manner as the writer in the *Analecta Ecclesiastica*. He lists a number of specific replies. On September 21, 1596, Carlinal Borromeo was told that public disputations between Catholics and heretics were to be avoided if this could be done without scandal. On August 13, 1609, the nuncio in Belgium was told to warn the religious superiors not to allow their subjects to enter into disputations with heretics unless they were very capable of defending the Catholic position. On October 22 of the same year it was stated that private conferences were not forbidden. Pignatelli admits that disputations were sometimes permitted, *e.g.*, in Westphalia on July 29, 1509, and Dec. 7, 1607.

---

[11] "Inter hereticos et catholicos disputationes fuerunt semper denegatae, quia ex ipsis nulla hauritur utilitas. Aliquando fuerunt concessae ad effectum convertendi."—III (1895), 297. Specific replies are reported for the years 1596, 1599 and 1653.

[12] The *Analecta Ecclesiastica* is the only available source from which a knowledge of these documents could be obtained. It is not possible, therefore, to give the exact wording or the exact date.

[13] *Consultationes*, t. I, c. XLV.

Ferraris [14] gives the same general conclusions, and he too lists specific replies of the Sacred Congregations. On February 26, 1630, the Sacred Congregation for the Propagation of the Faith stated that disputations in matters of faith were forbidden to lay people. Priests were counseled to avoid disputations unless they themselves were very learned. Ferraris says that when in the year 1635 some missionaries entered into disputations at Constantinople, their Superiors were warned not to permit public disputations again under pain of penalties to be inflicted by the Holy Office.[15] He also quotes a reply of the Sacred Congregation for the Propagation of the Faith under date of January 18, 1654, in which a missionary in Armenia is warned to refrain from disputing with the Armenian Patriarch concerning the two natures in Christ. Finally, he notes a reply under date of May 27, 1644, in which a missionary priest is reprimanded for having called his own ecclesiastical assemblage for the purpose of disputing with heretics. He was reprimanded for having done this without the permission of the Holy See.[16]

According to Bucceroni (1841-1918)[17] the same prohibition against holding disputations without papal permission was contained in decrees of the Sacred Congregation of the Council under date of March 6, 1625, and of the Holy Office under date of January 19, 1644.[18]

The reports in the *Analecta Ecclesiastica* and in the works of Pignatelli, Ferraris and Bucceroni are in conformity with the decrees of the Sacred Congregation for the Propagation of the Faith

---

[14] "Fides," n. 67.

[15] "Sanctissimus mandavit, significari Generalibus Regularium Perae commorantium, ut illis interdicerent, ne huiusmodi congressus aut disputationes publicas in posterum facere praesumerent sub poenis arbitrio S. C. Inquisitionis."

A response of the Sacred Congregation for the Propagation of the Faith very similar to this one quoted by Ferraris is noted by Loiselet as having been issued in the year 1631.—"Ce que pense l'Église des conférences contradictoires" —*Etudes*, CIV (1905), 482.

[16] The work of Ferraris is the only available source from which a knowledge of these documents could be obtained.

[17] *Enchiridion Morale* (4. ed., Romae, 1905), p. 52.

[18] The work of Bucceroni is the only available source from which a knowledge of these two documents could be obtained.

which are listed in the *Fontes*. In a reply of March 8, 1625, this Sacred Congregation made it clear that as a rule disputations with heretics were to be forbidden because the proponents of heretical opinions frequently made it appear that their teaching was the true one. If in certain cases it seemed necessary to hold disputations, the Sacred Congregation was to be informed, and it would prescribe under what conditions the disputations were to be held according to the circumstances in each particular case.[19]

In a reply under date of February 7, 1645, attention is drawn to the fact that formal disputations are licit when there is really hope of a greater good resulting, and when the other conditions set down by theologians are fulfilled. The controversies of St. Augustine with the heretics of his time are given as examples of licit formal disputations. The Sacred Congregation then goes on to say that the Holy See has frequently prohibited these disputations and counseled her ministers to do the same, because too often in the past they have been without profit to the Church and at times have been even injurious. If it seems necessary to hold disputations, the permission of the Holy See must be obtained. Furthermore, only learned men who are truly capable of defending the Catholic Faith shall take part in these disputations.[20]

---

[19] "S. Congregatio iussit publicas disputationes non fieri cum haereticis, quia plerumque vel ob loquacitatem vel audaciam aut circumstantis populi acclamationes veritas falsitate praevalente opprimitur; et si aliquando huiusmodi disputationes excusari non possint, primum de illis certior fiat S. Congregatio, quae iuxta temporis et personarum qualitatem quid agendum sit praescribit."— *Codicis Iuris Canonici Fontes cura Eṁi. Petri Card. Gasparri Editi* (9 vols., Romae [postea Civitate Vaticana]: Typis Polyglottis Vaticanis, 1923-1939 [Vols. VII-IX ed. *cura et studio Eṁi. Iustiniani Card. Serédi*]), n. 4428. Hereafter this work will be cited as *Fontes*.

[20] "Colloquia et disputationes publicas Catholicorum cum haereticis aliquando esse licitas, cum scilicet spes habetur maioris boni, et concurrunt aliae conditiones quae a theologis recensentur, ut patet ex iis disputationibus quas habuit S. Augustinus contra Donatistas et alios haereticos.

"Sanctam Sedem Apostolicam et Romanos Pontifices, quod huiusmodi colloquia, disputationes, et collationes plerumque sine bono, aut etiam cum malo exitu peracta fuerunt, illa frequenter prohibuisse, ac suis ministris scripsisse ut illa impedirent: si vero non possent impediri, curarent ne fierent sine auctoritate Apostolica, insisterentque ut per viros doctos, qui possent et valerent defendere

These same conclusions are briefly related in a reply of December 18, 1662.[21]

These decrees of the Sacred Congregation in listing the dangers involved in formal disputations follow very much the same line of reasoning as the commentators on the *Liber Sextus*. However, two new provisions are added which are worthy of note. First, as a general rule, both clerics and lay people are forbidden to take part in these disputations. The law of the *Liber Sextus*, as has been seen, did not forbid the participation of clerics. Secondly, a formal disputation was not to be held without the permission of the Holy See.

Only public disputations are referred to in these decrees of the Sacred Congregation, but lay people were still forbidden to participate in private disputations by reason of the law of the *Liber Sextus* which remained in force until the advent of the Code. Finally, it should be noted that both the law of the *Liber Sextus* and the decrees of the Sacred Congregation apparently did not apply to non-Catholics other than heretics.

In view of these explicit declarations of the Sacred Congregation for the Propagation of the Faith, it is difficult to understand the legislation of several particular councils which took place during the eighteenth and nineteenth centuries. In a synod held by the Maronites at Mount Lebanon in 1736 it was decreed that no one was to enter into a public disputation with heretics or infidels unless he had previously received the express permission of the ordinary, who was to grant permission only to those who were conspicuous for their learning and piety.[22] At a Plenary Council of the

veritates Catholicas id perageretur, et saepissime id ipsum S. C. de Prop. Fide rescripsit ad suos missionarios eosque monuit ut a publicis disputationibus cum haereticis abstinerent."—*Fontes*, n. 4457.

[21] "De conferentiis et publicis congressibus seu disputationibus missionariorum cum haereticis monetur Generalis (Capuccin.) ut omnino prohibeat, cum S. Sedes plurimis experimentis edocta semper eas prohibuerit; quo vero ad interventum concionibus haereticorum, hoc etiam prohibeatur, sicut a S. C. S. Officii semper fuit prohibitum, nec omnibus indifferenter absolute expediat; quod si aliquis adsit insignioris doctrinae et prudentiae supplicet in particulari pro licentia."—*Fontes*, n. 4467.

[22] "N. 7—De fidei dogmatibus cum haereticis aut infidelibus publice dis-

Bishops of Ireland, held at Thurles in the year 1850, it was stated that both clerics and lay people were forbidden to participate in public disputations with non-Catholics unless they had previously received the permission of the ordinary.[23]   In the legislation concerning disputations of the diocesan synod held at Bahia, Brazil, in the year 1707, it was simply asserted that disputations in matters of faith were to be avoided by lay people.[24]

In none of these particular councils is explicit mention made of the necessity of having recourse to the Holy See in each particular case.   As regards the synod of the Maronites, this provision is implicitly excluded since it is stated in the decrees of this synod that the ordinary may grant the necessary permission to those who are conspicuous for their learning and piety.   It is possible that this provision was implicitly included in the Plenary Council of the Bishops of Ireland, since the law of this Council did not expressly state that the ordinary could grant the required permission without having had recourse to the Holy See.   If the words of the law are accepted at their face value, however, it must be concluded that here, too, the decrees of the Sacred Congregation for the Propagation of the Faith were overlooked.   In the Synod of Bahia it is not even stated that the permission of the ordinary is required, nor is anything said concerning clerical participation in disputations.

These decrees of the Sacred Congregation for the Propagation of the Faith were certainly *de jure* in effect in the United States during the nineteenth century.   Whether or not they were *de facto*

---

putare nemo praesumat sine expressa Ordinarii licentia, quae illis tantum erit concedenda, quos noverit sufficienti doctrina praeditos et in religione Catholica constantes."—*Acta et Decreta Sanctorum Conciliorum Recentiorum, Collectio Lacensis* (7 vols., Friburgi Brisgoviae, 1870-1890), II, 100B.   Hereafter this work will be referred to as *Collectio Lacensis.*

[23] LX, *De fidei periculis evitandis,* n. 7: "Catholicos laicos cum acatholicis hortamur de rebus ad religionem pertinentibus non agere.   Vetamus ne publice, absque Ordinarii licentia, ab aliquo, sive clerico sive laico, cum iisdem disputationes ineantur; quippe ex eiusmodi disceptationibus vix quidquam boni fructus expectari potest, et ferme semper accidit.ut Christiana pax et caritas violentur." —*Collectio Lacensis,* III, 777.

[24] *Collectio Lacensis,* I, 850A.

observed is a moot question. No mention is made of the decrees, nor is there any legislation concerning disputations, in the provincial or plenary councils of Baltimore, or in the diocesan synods and provincial councils listed in the *Collectio Lacensis*.[25] It is quite possible that the decrees were not always observed in the United States during this period inasmuch as the necessity of defending the faith may have frequently forced Catholics to participate in formal disputations on very short notice.

Despite the apparent non-observance of the decrees in particular localities, however, the practice of the Church as revealed in these decrees of the Sacred Congregation has remained unchanged up to the present time. This fact is witnessed by several recent pronouncements.

In a letter to Cardinal Gibbons, in the year 1899, Leo XIII (1878-1903) touches the question of disputations while pointing out the methods to be used in gaining converts. After saying that the principal work of the clergy in this regard consists in preaching, he adds:

> Quod si, e diversis rationibus verbi Dei eloquendi, ea quandoque praeferenda videatur, qua ad dissidentes non in templis dicant sed privato quovis loco, nec ut qui disputent sed ut qui amice colloquantur, res quidem reprehensione caret; modo tamen ad id muneris auctoritate episcoporum ii destinentur, qui scientiam integritatemque suam antea ipsis probaverint.[26]

On January 27, 1902, the decrees of the Sacred Congregation for the Propagation of the Faith of the years 1625 and 1645, which forbade disputations with heretics, were applied to disputations with Socialists by the Sacred Congregation for Extraordinary Affairs.[27]

---

[25] Vol. III.

[26] *"Testem benevolentiae,"* 22 ian. 1899, n. 13—*Fontes*, n. 640.

[27] N. 8: "Contenendo le dottrine socialistiche nel loro complesso delle vere eresie, id cosidetti *contradditori* coi socialisti vanno soggeti ai decreti della Santa Sede relativi alle publiche dispute cogli eretici. Il decreto della S. C. di Propaganda Fide de Febbraio 7, 1645, riassume in questa forma la legislazione sempre vigente in tale materia.

(Here the decree is quoted *verbatim*.)

"E uno dei motivi, per i quali la Santa Sede ha proibito tali publiche dispute

The reason given was that many Socialist teachings are heretical. It is asserted in this reply that the legislation concerning disputations has always been in effect.

This Instruction, as such, at the time of its original publication affected Italy alone. It interpreted the decrees of the Sacred Congregation for the Propagation of the Faith as forbidding disputations with all non-Catholics (therefore not only heretics) insofar as the disputations embraced *ex professo* any point which is heretical. The significance of this interpretation will be discussed in the following chapter.

In the Plenary Council of Latin America (1899)[28] and the I Plenary Council of Quebec (1909)[29] laws were promulgated which summarized the teaching set forth by the Sacred Congregations. Both laws conclude with a clause forbidding any cleric to take part in public formal disputations without having first consulted the ordinary. The ordinary in such cases is to seek a norm of acting from the Holy See.

è accennato in altro decreto dell' 8 marzo 1625 con queste parole, che hanno anche oggi una dolorosa attualità: 'Perchè spesso o la falsa eloquenza, o l'audacia od il genere di uditorio fanno sì che l'errore applaudito trionfi sulla verità.' "— *Fontes,* n. 6416.

[28] "Quamvis certum sit disputationes publicas catholicorum cum haereticis aliquando esse licitas, cum scilicet spes habeatur maioris boni, et concurrant aliae conditiones quae a theologis recensentur; tamen sciendum est Sanctam Sedem Apostolicam et Romanos Pontifices, ad omnem imprudentiam et temeritatem in re tanti momenti impediendam, illas frequenter prohibuisse; plerumque enim, ob loquacitatem vel audaciam aut circumstantias populi acclamantis, veritas, falsitate praevalente, opprimitur (1625, 1662, 1674, 1899). Igitur nullus e clero praesumat huiusmodi publicas disputationes instituere, inconsulto episcopo, qui iuxta normas a Sancta Sede praescriptas procedet."—*Acta et Decreta Concilii Plenarii Americae Latinae in Urbe Celebrati A. D., MDCCCXCIX* (Romae: Typis Vaticanis, 1902), n. 145.

[29] "Disputatio cum haereticis—Laici, qui per medios haereticos vitam civilem ducunt, temere cum illis ad dicendum de re religiosa non aggrediantur. Item, licet catholicorum cum acatholicis disputationes publice possint certis sub conditionibus in bonum vergere, ne tamen veritas adversis circumstantiis opprimatur, nullus e clero praesumat disputationes easdem instituere, inconsulto episcopo, cuius erit agendi normam a S. Sede expetere."—*Acta et Decreta Concilii Plenarii Quebecensis Primi Anno Domini MCMIX* (Quebeci: typis "L'action Sociale Limitée," 1912), n. 414.

CHAPTER IV

THE LEGISLATION OF THE CODE

Canon 1325, § 3. Caveant catholici ne disputationes
..., publicas praesertim, cum acatholicis habeant, sine
venia Sanctae Sedis aut, si casus urgeat, loci Ordinarii.

ARTICLE 1. THE OBJECT OF THE LAW

IT IS clear from the historical background and from the words
of the legislator that only formal disputations are the object of the
law.[1] Material disputations are not comprehended, for these are
held between Catholics, and the law speaks only of disputations between Catholics and non-Catholics. Dubitative disputations are not
comprehended, for from the text of the law it is clear that the
disputations under discussion can be licit. Dubitative disputations
can never be licit, and thus not even the Holy See could allow Catholics to participate in them.

The law has in view formal debates arranged beforehand, not
discussions or controversies which arise extemporaneously in the
course of a conversation or meeting.[2] This distinction seems to be
valid, for if a person becomes involved in an extemporaneous formal
disputation, whether public or private, he will of necessity have to
judge immediately for himself according to the principles of the
natural law whether or not such participation is licit. With regard
to apologetic conferences, round-table discussions, etc., it can be
stated that as a general rule they are not affected by the law insofar

---

[1] It is suggested that the reader review the preliminary notions given at the
beginning of the first part of the present work.

[2] Ayrinhac, *Administrative Legislation in the New Code of Canon Law* (New
York: Longmans, Green & Co., 1930), n. 165; De Meester, *Juris Canonici et
Juris Canonico-Civilis Compendium* (nova editio, ad normam codicis juris
canonici, 3 vols. in 4, Brugis: Desclée de Brouwer et Socii, 1921-1928), n. 1284.
Hereafter the work of Ayrinhac will be cited as *Administrative Legislation* and
the work of De Meester as *Compendium*.

as it deals with disputations, the reason being that they do not partake of the nature of a debate.

A written controversy, even though it has all the elements of a disputation except that it is not oral, does not come under the law.[3] However, the legislation of the Code regarding the censure and prohibition of books will have its effect upon such a controversy. The Catholic party could not publish his arguments without the permission of his superiors.[4] On the other hand, Catholics would be forbidden to read the arguments of the non-Catholic party,[5] unless they had previously received permission to do so from the proper authorities.[6]

Moreover, as is evident from the context (which is concerned with the ecclesiastical *magisterium*) and the historical background, the law deals only with disputations in matters of faith. This means that disputations with non-Catholics on such topics as social reconstruction, labor unions, etc., are not forbidden unless one or more of the dogmas of faith are professedly included in the topic of debate.

At first sight it may appear that a general norm is established in the Instruction published by the Sacred Congregation for Extraordinary Ecclesiastical Affairs [7] whereby all public disputations with non-Catholics are prohibited, no matter what the topic of debate may be. However, upon close consideration of the Instruction, it becomes evident that disputations with Socialists and other non-Catholics are forbidden only insofar as they come under the decrees of the Sacred Congregation for the Propagation of the Faith, which decrees in turn forbid disputations with non-Catholics only insofar as these disputations embrace *ex professo* any particular point which is heretical.

---

[3] Ayrinhac, *Administrative Legislation*, n. 165; Vermeersch, *Theologiae Moralis Principia-Responsa-Concilia* (3. ed., 4 vols., Romae: Università Gregoriana, 1933), II, 52. Hereafter this work will be cited as *Theologiae Moralis Principia*.

[4] Canon 1385.

[5] Canons 1384, 1399.

[6] Canon 1402.

[7] Cf. *supra*, p. 29, footnote 27.

The words *"publicas praesertim"* indicate that public disputations constitute a more serious problem than private disputations. The reasons for this are: first, the element of an audience must be considered in the determination of the morality of a public disputation; second, a Catholic may participate in a public disputation only if he has a canonical mission from his ecclesiastical superiors.

The question is: are private disputations forbidden in any way by the law of the Code, or is the morality of participation in such disputations to be decided solely according to the principles of the natural law?

The interpretation of a few of the commentators of the text [8] could easily lead one to believe that sometimes, but not always, permission must be sought for participation in private disputations. Such an interpretation, however, would at one and the same time include private disputations within the object of the law and yet destroy the force of the law in their regard, for the decision as to whether or not permission is required would be left to the individual participant in each particular case. De Meester takes a more positive stand.

> Dicitur tamen *praesertim publicas* prohiberi, inde concluditur privatas disputationes aut collationes non tantum jure naturae sed etiam aliquando jure ecclesiastico vetari, pro rei et adjunctorum momento, ubi religionis specialiter intersit, de quibus judicium est penes auctoritatem ecclesiasticam.[9]

He apparently maintains that all private disputations are subject to the approval of the ecclesiastical authorities, for despite his verbal distinction, if private disputations are sometimes forbidden by ecclesiastical law by reason of the topic and the circumstances, how else can this be effected except by previous censorship of all disputations on the part of the ecclesiastical authorities?

---

[8] Wernz-Vidal, *Ius Canonicum ad Codicis Normam Exactum* (7 vols. in 8, Romae: apud Aedes Universitatis Gregorianae, 1923-1938), Tom. IV, n. 619; Ayrinhac, *Administrative Legislation*, n. 165; Blat, *Commentarium Textus Codicis Iuris Canonici* (6 vols., Romae: ex Typographia Pontificis in Instituto Pii IX, 1921-1927), IV, n. 199. Hereafter the work of Wernz-Vidal will be cited as *Ius Canonicum* and the work of Blat as *Commentarium*.

[9] *Compendium*, n. 1284.

Bouscaren [10] states clearly that in his opinion private disputations are not forbidden by the law of the Code. He explains that the Code uses language which elegantly insinuates that even private disputations are not to be undertaken without hope of advantage, and that the natural law requires certain conditions which must be fulfilled, but he maintains that the strict canonical requisite of permission from the Holy See does not apply to them. In support of his opinion he cites Vermeersch-Creusen [11] and Coronata.[12]

This opinion of Bouscaren has the quality of clearness, but it appears to be too broad an interpretation of the law. While it is certainly true that public disputations are especially emphasized in the text of the law, it is equally true that private disputations are included within the object of the law. But if this be so, it must be admitted that they are prohibited unless permission to participate in them has been obtained from the Holy See when this is possible. The fact that Gasparri, in the footnotes of his edition of the Code, cites only laws which treat of public disputations, does not detract from the truth of this conclusion. The words of the law are sufficiently clear to indicate that an element has been added to the law of the Code which was not contained in these previous pronouncements.

It is maintained, therefore, that *per se* the strict canonical requisite of permission from the Holy See applies to both public and private disputations. However, because of the distinction made between the two types of disputations in the law it seems reasonable to state that a lesser cause would suffice for the granting of permission to participate in a private disputation. Thus, in relation to private disputations, the clause *"si casus urgeat"* would be more easily verified, and when even the ordinary of the place cannot be reached, a lesser cause would justify participation in a private disputation without permission.

[10] "Cooperation with Non-Catholics, Canonical Legislation," *Theological Studies*, III (1942), 505.

[11] *Epitome Iuris Canonici* (3 vols. [Vol. I, 5. ed., 1934; Vol. II, 5. ed., 1936; Vol. III, 6. ed., 1937], Mechliniae-Romae: H. Dessain), II, n. 661. Hereafter this work will be cited as *Epitome*.

[12] *Institutiones Iuris Canonici* (5 vols. [Vols. I et II, 2. ed.], Taurini: Marietti, 1933-1939), n. 912. Hereafter this work will be cited as *Institutiones*.

It must be kept in mind that private discussions between Catholics and non-Catholics are not ordinarily prearranged formal disputations. A person who is a prospective convert or who is merely seeking information can scarcely be said to be disputing. On the other hand, when all the elements are present which are necessary to constitute a private prearranged formal disputation, the conditions required by the natural law for licit Catholic participation in such a discussion will only rarely be present. In fine, while it must be said the private disputations are comprehended within the law, the conditions will rarely be present which would justify one's seeking permission from the Holy See to participate in such a disputation.

The decrees of the Sacred Congregation for the Propagation of the Faith [18] treat of disputations with heretics, while the Code speaks of disputations with all non-Catholics. Even though from the earliest days of the Church the word "heretic" has been used to signify but one type of non-Catholic, namely, a person who has received baptism and retains the Christian name, but who denies one or more of the revealed truths, there are good reasons for upholding the opinion that there is no difference between the law of the Code and the decrees as regards this particular point. These are: first, the reasons given by the Sacred Congregation in prohibiting disputations are equally applicable to all non-Catholics, whether they be heretics, apostates, schismatics, or infidels; secondly, the interpretation of these decrees as given by the Sacred Congregation for Extraordinary Ecclesiastical Affairs indicates that they referred to disputations with all non-Catholics.

According to the decree of the Sacred Congregation for Extraordinary Ecclesiastical Affairs 'issued on January 27, 1902, "Since the tenets of Socialism, taken in their entirety, contain real heresies, those who are called the 'Contradictors of Socialists' come under the decrees of the Holy See regarding public disputations with heretics." As was mentioned in the previous chapter, in the light of these words it must be concluded that the decrees of the Sacred Congregation for the Propagation of the Faith prohibited disputations not only with heretics but with all non-Catholics insofar as the disputation embraced *ex professo* any particular point which is

---

[18] *Fontes,* nn. 4428, 4457, 4467.

heretical. Thus, according to the decrees of the Sacred Congregation and the law of the Code, Catholics may not participate with non-Catholics in disputations, whether the non-Catholics be heretics, apostates, schismatics, Jews or infidels.

In fine, canon 1325, § 3, forbids Catholics to participate with non-Catholics in oral, prearranged, formal debates on matters of faith unless they have previously obtained permission to do so from the proper ecclesiastical authorities.

ARTICLE 2. THE SUBJECTS OF THE LAW

All Catholics, according to the Code, whether they be clerics, religious, or lay people, are forbidden to participate in disputations with non-Catholics. This extensive prohibition is a change from the law of the *Liber Sextus*, wherein only the laity were forbidden to participate in formal disputations.[14] The present law, however, is but a renewal of the prohibitions laid down by the various Sacred Congregations since the time of the Reformation.

Certainly all Catholics of the Latin Church are bound by the law. Oriental Catholics are at least required to seek permission from the ordinary of the place, for, as will be shown in Article 4 of this Chapter, no person may licitly participate in a public formal disputation unless he has obtained a canonical mission from the proper ecclesiastical authorities. It seems, too, that Oriental Catholics are bound by the law insofar as it posits the necessity of obtaining permission from the Holy See when this is possible. This law is not a purely disciplinary measure, but a means of safeguarding Catholics from the taint of heresy, and as such, according to canon 1, it is binding on Oriental Catholics.

ARTICLE 3. SUPERIORS FROM WHOM PERMISSION IS TO BE OBTAINED

According to the law of the Code, Catholics may not participate in formal disputations unless they have first obtained permission from the Holy See or, in urgent cases, from the ordinary of the place. Since there is nothing in the nature of the question or in

---

[14] C. 2, *de haereticis*, V, 2, in VI°.

the wording of the law to suggest that the personal intervention of the Supreme Pontiff is required, it can be concluded that the term "Holy See" is here used to designate one of the Sacred Congregations.[15] Moreover, since the law is directly concerned with matters of faith, it is obvious that the required permission is to be obtained from the Sacred Congregation of the Holy Office.[16] A person directly subject to the Sacred Congregation of Religious, to the Sacred Congregation for the Propagation of the Faith, or to the Sacred Oriental Congregation, may seek the necessary permission through these Congregations, but they in turn will have to refer the matter to the Holy Office.[17]

There is no difficulty in understanding why in the past the Sacred Congregation for the Propagation of the Faith and the Sacred Congregation for Extraordinary Ecclesiastical Affairs have handed down decisions in this matter. When the Sacred Congregation for the Propagation of the Faith was instituted by Gregory XV in 1622[18] it was given very broad power over the territories and persons subject to it. This Congregation was under no obligation to refer questions of faith to the Holy Office. Thus it is understandable why the Sacred Congregation for the Propagation of the Faith handed down decisions concerning disputations in 1625, 1645 and 1662.[19] It was not until 1908 that its competence was restricted. In that year, Pius X, in the Constitution *"Sapienti consilio,"* set forth that the Sacred Congregation for the Propagation of the Faith was not to transact business relating to the faith. Thenceforth when any such question was proposed to this Congregation it was to be referred to the Holy Office.[20] Since these provisions of the Constitution *"Sapienti consilio"* are retained in the Code,[21] it is clear that the Sacred Congregation for the Propagation of the Faith is no longer competent to give permission for participation in disputations.

[15] Canon 7.
[16] Canon 247, § 1.
[17] Canons 251, § 2; 252, § 4; 257, § 2.
[18] Const. *"Inscrutabili"—Fontes,* n. 199.
[19] *Fontes,* nn. 4428, 4457, 4467.
[20] Const. *"Sapienti consilio,"* 29 iun. 1908—*Fontes,* n. 682.
[21] Canon 252, § 4.

Certainly since the year 1814 the Sacred Congregation for Extraordinary Ecclesiastical Affairs has been empowered to handle matters which were submitted to its examination by the Supreme Pontiff through the Cardinal Secretary of State. The competence of this Congregation varies with each commission it receives from the Holy See. Since its competence may be very extensive in a particular case, there is no difficulty in understanding its decision concerning disputations with Socialists.[22]

When there is danger in delay and the Holy See cannot be reached, the ordinary of the place may grant permission for a Catholic to participate in a formal disputation. In a broad sense this provision of the law may be said to be a particular application of canon 81. Although the permission in question is not a dispensation strictly so-called, still both laws appear to be governed by the same principle. Thus the ordinary of the place could not grant the required permission unless the conditions analogous to those stated in canon 81 were present. In other words, the ordinary of the place could not of his own accord allow a Catholic to participate in a formal disputation unless it were prudently foreseen that the postponement of this disputation until such time as the permission of the Holy See could be obtained would result in grave harm to the Church.

These conditions are not nearly so formidable as they may at first seem, for in practice, once it is granted that recourse cannot be had to the Holy See, the ordinary of the place could grant a Catholic permission to participate in any formal disputation in which there is a well-founded hope that the net results of the disputation will be beneficial to the cause of Christ. This is so because the failure to take advantage of this well-founded hope would necessarily involve a danger of grave harm to the Church.

Granted that recourse cannot be had to the Holy See and that there is danger in delay, permission to participate in formal disputations is to be obtained from the ordinary of the place where the disputation is to be held. With the exception of major superiors in clerical exempt religious institutes all those enumerated in canon 198, § 1, are ordinaries of places.

---

[22] N. 8—*Fontes*, n. 6416.

With regard to his own proper subjects, the decision as to whether or not permission should be granted will rest entirely with the ordinary of the place. By analogy with the legislation on preaching it seems that a religious would need the consent of his superior before he could take advantage of the permission obtained from the ordinary of the place.[23] So too it seems that the ordinary of the place could not grant permission to a layman or priest from another diocese unless he had first obtained the necessary credentials from the proper ordinary of the person in question.[24]

There could arise a case wherein a Catholic, if he were not able to have recourse to the Holy See or to the local ordinary, would have to decide for himself whether or not he could licitly participate in a particular formal disputation. Under such circumstances the law would cease, and he could take part in the disputation, if it were prudently foreseen that the postponement of this disputation until such time as the higher ecclesiastical authorities could be reached would result in grave harm to the Church.

ARTICLE 4. THE REASONS FOR SEEKING PERMISSION

The office of preaching the Catholic faith is committed especially to the Roman Pontiff for the Universal Church, and to the bishops for their respective dioceses.[25] Moreover, no one is allowed to exercise the ministry of preaching, unless he has received a canonical mission to do so.[26] These laws of the Code are not simply disciplinary measures. They flow from the very constitution of the Church. The sacred deposit of revealed truth has been entrusted by Christ to a permanent and official teaching body. By divine right the Roman Pontiff for the Universal Church and the bishops for their respective dioceses are the administrators of this supernatural deposit. No other person has the right publicly to explain or defend the truths contained therein unless he has first obtained the authorization of these official guardians. It is the office and the duty of the Roman Pontiff and of the bishops to spread the knowl-

[23] Canon 1339, § 2.
[24] Canon 1341, § 1.
[25] Canon 1327.
[26] Canon 1328.

edge of these truths and to defend them when necessary. All others who take up this work do so only by virtue of a participation in the episcopal office.

These principles are the foundations upon which the laws concerning the giving of catechetical instruction [27] and the preaching of sermons [28] are based. These principles, moreover, are the fundamental guides in the understanding of any laws or regulations which concern a public exposition or defense of the faith.

Thus it seems clear why Catholics, before they may participate in public disputations or conferences with non-Catholics on religious matters, must have the permission of at least the local ordinary. Such participation involves an exposition of the faith which is generically the same as that entailed in the giving of catechetical instructions and the preaching of sermons, and it requires, therefore, a special canonical mission.[29]

From this it follows that the necessity of seeking permission for participation in public disputations and conferences on matters of faith is not simply a disciplinary measure. It is a necessary consequence flowing from the public law of the Church. This conclusion helps to clear up two important questions. First, it means that Oriental Catholics are also bound by the law at least insofar as the permission of the local ordinary is required for participation in public disputations. Secondly, it means that public conferences on religious matters, as opposed to disputations strictly so-called, do come under the law because participation in these conferences necessarily entails a public exposition of faith.[30]

Even granted, however, that the matter of the law, at least insofar as it treats of public disputations, is a public question, this only explains the law insofar as it requires at least the permission of the local ordinary for participation in such disputations. The question still remains as to why the local ordinary can grant permission only in urgent cases, inasmuch as in all other cases the matter is reserved

----

[27] Canons 1329-1336.

[28] Canons 1337-1348.

[29] De Meester, *Compendium*, n. 1284; Wernz-Vidal, *Ius Canonicum*, Tom. IV, n. 619.

[30] For a more detailed treatment of this point, see pp. 69-70.

to the Holy See. The problem is obviously a *causa maior*, i. e., a matter of such great importance that it is reserved to the Roman Pontiff either by its nature or by positive law.[31]

Matters which are reserved to the Roman Pontiff by their nature are *causae maiores*, either *essentiales* or *per se*. *Causae maiores essentiales* embrace those matters for which the ordinary power of the residential bishop is essentially inadequate, precisely because they are only relatively diocesan in as far as they apply antecedently to and irrespective of any territorial division of the Universal Church. They include those matters which require infallibility of doctrine and which are contained in the dogmatic laws subsequent to it, as well as those purely disciplinary laws which concern the status of the Universal Church. *Causae maiores per se* are those which arise consequent to the territorial division of the Church from the relation of the individual dioceses to the central authority or of one diocese to another. Matters which are reserved to the Roman Pontiff by positive law are called *causae maiores per accidens*. Such matters are potentially subject to the bishop's jurisdiction, yet have been actually subjected by positive ecclesiastical legislation to the higher authority of the Pope.[32]

The granting of permission to participate in a public formal disputation is obviously not a *causa maior per se*. With equal certainty it can be said that it is not to be included among those matters which require infallibility of doctrine or which are contained in the dogmatic laws subsequent to this infallibility. Finally, although this law does, in a sense, affect every person in the Church, it seems impossible to prove that *de iure* the intervention of the Holy See is necessary for the preservation of the principle embodied in the law. A final argument to prove that this matter is not a *causa maior essentialis* or a *causa maior per se* is the fact that the granting of permission to participate in formal public disputations was never reserved during the first sixteen centuries of the Church's existence.

---

[31] Canon 220.

[32] Ryan, *Principles of Episcopal Jurisdiction*, The Catholic University of America Canon Law Studies, n. 120 (Washington, D. C.: The Catholic University of America Press, 1939), pp. 66-67, 91-92.

It remains, then, that this matter is reserved to the Roman Pontiff by positive law, and it is therefore a *causa maior per accidens*. It is potentially subject to the bishop's jurisdiction, yet has been actually subjected by positive ecclesiastical legislation to the higher authority of the Pope. The reason is briefly this: granted that public formal disputations are licit in themselves and in their purpose, the circumstances requisite for licitness are rarely present; and therefore the Holy See wishes to control the circumstances by requiring special permission in every case.[33]

As has been pointed out, the fundamental legal reason why a Catholic may not participate in a public formal disputation without having first obtained the permission of at least the local ordinary is that such participation requires a canonical mission. It should be noted, however, that the decrees of the Sacred Congregations and the commentators (both of the *Liber Sextus* and of the Code) do not lay great stress on this legal reason. They explain the necessity of the law chiefly on moral grounds, for example, because of the danger that, either by reason of the loquacity and boldness of the adversaries or the acclamations of the crowd, the truth will be shouted down and falsehood will prevail. The fact that the permission of the Holy See is required—since the necessity of this step cannot be proved from the constitution of the Church—is further reason for saying that disputations are considered as a separate entity in the Code, not because of any canonical mission involved, but because they are fraught with dangers for Catholic participants and listeners.

The inclusion of private disputations within the object of the law is also best explained on moral, rather than legal, grounds. When all the elements are present which are necessary to constitute a private prearranged formal disputation the dangers involved in such a discussion will ordinarily far outweigh the possible good results to be expected. Thus, in order to safeguard the faith of her children, the Church has deemed it necessary to prohibit Catholics from participating in private disputations, unless permission to

---

[33] Bouscaren, "Cooperation with Non-Catholics, Canonical Legislation," *Theological Studies*, III (1942), 504.

do so has been obtained from the Holy See or, in urgent cases, from the local ordinary.

ARTICLE 5. PUNISHMENTS

The only punishment enacted by the general law previous to the Code was the *ferendae sententiae* penalty of the *Liber Sextus* whereby the punishment of excommunication was to be meted out to those lay people who entered into formal disputations, whether public or private, without having first obtained the permission of the proper ecclesiastical authorities. This punishment has been abrogated by the Code.[34]

Although no specific penalty is enacted by the Code for those who participate in formal disputations without permission, such persons could, nevertheless, be punished by the ordinary in virtue of canon 2222, § 1. This is so because a person who would knowingly and wilfully perform a given act without having first obtained the required permission of the Holy See would necessarily be guilty of an especially grave transgression of the law. Moreover, scandal could very easily arise if it were publicly known that the disputation was entered into without permission.

[34] Canon 6, 5°.

CONCLUSIONS AND SUMMARY

1. Of the three types of disputations, material, dubitative, and formal, only dubitative disputations are absolutely prohibited by the natural law. Material and formal disputations are in themselves licit. Prescinding from ecclesiastical legislation, the licitness of any particular material or formal disputation will be determined by a consideration of the intentions of the participants, the audience, the object, the circumstances and the end of the disputation.

2. Ecclesiastical legislation concerning material disputations has been confined to an explanation of the provisions of the natural law as affecting such disputations. The prohibition of the natural law against dubitative disputations has been explicitly promulgated by the Church since the first days of her existence.

3. The first legislation treating of formal disputations appeared in the thirteenth century when according to the law of the *Liber Sextus* lay people were forbidden to participate in public or private formal disputations. The violators of this law, which was in force until the advent of the Code, were subject to the *ferendae sententiae* penalty of excommunication.

4. The next development came after the Protestant Revolt, that is, in the seventeenth, or possibly the sixteenth century. At that time all Catholics, clerics and lay people, were forbidden to participate in public formal disputations unless they had previously received permission to do so from the Holy See.

5. According to canon 1325, § 3, all Catholics are forbidden to participate in formal disputations (prearranged oral debates on matters of faith with heretics, schismatics, apostates, Jews or infidels) unless they have previously received permission to do so from the Holy Office or, in urgent cases, from the ordinary of the place where the disputation is to be held. The law ceases to bind if in a given case even the ordinary of the place cannot be reached.

6. Insofar as it prescribes the necessity of obtaining the permission of the local ordinary for participation in public disputations, the law of the Code is but a necessary consequence of the consti-

tutional law of the Church, according to which no Catholic may publicly expose or defend the truths of faith unless he has previously received permission to do so from the official custodians of those truths. As regards the necessity of obtaining the permission of the Holy See, it seems that the matter is only a *causa maior per accidens*, that is, while it is potentially subject to the bishop's jurisdiction, it has been actually subjected by positive ecclesiastical legislation to the higher authority of the Pope. The inclusion of private disputations within the object of the law constitutes a disciplinary measure on the part of the Chuch to safeguard the faith of her children.

Part II

Conferences

PRELIMINARY NOTIONS

A conference, for present purposes, may be described as any discussion of a formal nature between Catholics and non-Catholics other than a formal disputation. Such a meeting differs specifically from a disputation in that the note of opposition between the parties involved (which characterizes disputations) is altogether lacking. There is no question of one group trying to overcome the other by force of argument or rhetoric.

Only those conferences will be considered in which Catholics and non-Catholics participate as members of their respective religious bodies. Thus there will be no discussion of conferences in which Catholics and non-Catholics participate without paying any particular attention to their religious beliefs, as for example in meetings held by social or athletic clubs.

There are two fundamental types of conferences between religious bodies as such. One type is held for the specific and immediate purpose of bringing one or more non-Catholics into the true Church of Christ. Such a conference is of course good and laudable, yet before it can be entered into certain precautions must be taken lest there be any whittling down of dogmatic truths. In all other cases the religions involved preserve their peculiar identity before and after the conference. The mutual antagonism and rivalry of disputations are replaced by mutual collaboration and cooperation. With the recognition and acknowledgment of differences the members of the various religious groups strive for one end by means of common or parallel action.

Conferences of this second type have come into prominence during the nineteenth and twentieth centuries. They have been fostered by the conviction that a limited cooperation between the members of the various religious bodies is good and at times even necessary. This conviction derives from a number of causes: the necessary and frequent intermingling of Catholics and non-Catholics in daily life, the increased facilities of communication, the influence of education, the fear of a revival of the religious persecutions which have marked the history of the United States and other countries, the healthy reaction of all fair-minded people against the tactics of such organizations as the Ku Klux Klan and the American Protective Association, the growth of organizations which are diabolically opposed to the fundamental tenets held alike by all established religions, the realization that there can be no social or political unity without religious unity, the theory that a definite step will have been taken toward religious unity if there is unity (based on the natural law) in respect to moral, social, and political issues. Finally, the motive cause of many of these conferences has been the erroneous conviction that no one religion exists by divine right to the exclusion of all others. As will be readily understood, this conviction has frequently fostered, and in turn has been fostered by, the causes listed above.[1]

Conferences of this second type may be divided into three groups: (1) those which aim at a union of the churches with due allowance for particular differences; (2) those which strive for mutual tolerance without formal union, and (3) those which are concerned primarily with moral, social or civic issues.

The morality of Catholic participation in such conferences will be regulated by two basic principles.[2] The first is the law of fraternal charity. Regardless of his race, creed, or color, every man has a claim to the supernatural love of his fellow man because he is made to the image of God and is at least potentially the recipient of sanctifying grace. The second principle is the fundamental doctrine that Catholicism is the only true religion and that its acceptance is obligatory by divine law on all mankind. Thus a Catholic may not give positive approval or assistance to the propagation of

---

[1] Many of these causes are listed by Connell.—"Catholics and 'Inter-faith' Groups," *The Ecclesiastical Review*, CV (1941), 340. Neither list is intended to embrace all the possible causes.

[2] Connell, *ibidem*, pp. 337-339.

a non-Catholic religion, for no religion but the Catholic religion has an objective right to exist in the light of the divine law.

Wisdom and prudence are needed to balance properly the requirements of both principles, for undue emphasis on one can easily lead to the violation of the other. The Catholic who hates heresy may easily find himself hating the heretic; on the other hand, the Catholic who strives earnestly to be charitable toward his non-Catholic friends may easily become guilty of statements and conduct fostering the erroneous doctrines of indifferentism and liberalism.

In the light of these principles certain conclusions are evident. Participation in conferences which aim at a union of the churches with due allowance for particular differences, that is, on the basis of a lowest common denominator, is forbidden to Catholics. Participation in conferences which serve to promote tolerance, if they strive to imbue the participants with a respect for the diverse religions of others, is likewise forbidden to Catholics. There is but one true religion and there can be no tolerance of, much less respect for, religious beliefs opposed to it. The practical identity of the two types of conferences discussed in this paragraph is brought out by the responses of the Holy Office.[3]

On the other hand, participation in conferences which deal with moral, social, or civic issues, or which serve to promote a spirit of fraternal charity, may be licit to Catholics, provided that the danger of religious indifferentism has been sufficiently guarded against. Such participation may be laudable and even necessary when it is the best means that men of differing religious beliefs have of fighting a common foe. Catholics, however, must always be aware that the cooperation entailed in these conferences is but a secondary solution to the problems which exist today. Such cooperation is in itself licit only because the ideal solution, the union of all men within the Mystical Body of Christ, the Roman Catholic Church, is not practicable at the present time.

It has been said that religious indifferentism must be guarded against. The danger of a display of indifferentism is present in the very holding of such conferences, because to the onlooker at least

---

[3] These responses will be discussed at length in the following Chapter.

there is present a certain basis of equality among the various religions. Moreover, a great many non-Catholics have no conception of any one religion existing by divine right. Too often the opinion is voiced that it makes no difference whether a person belongs to this or that religion as long as he is sincere in his particular religious convictions and leads a good life. This air of indifference will naturally make itself felt at conferences in which these non-Catholics take part. The danger deriving from indifferentism is further augmented by the not infrequent erroneous statements of Catholics and non-Catholics alike as regards the relationships of the various religious groups.

It can be seen, therefore, that although a great amount of good is to be expected from these conferences, an equally great amount of evil is to be avoided. It can be understood, too, why the Church has proceeded cautiously in her regulations concerning Catholic participation in these conferences. These regulations are of particular interest to the canonist, to whom the problem presents a twofold question. Has the Church seen fit explicitly and absolutely to forbid Catholics from participating in one or more of these types of conferences? If, and when, participation in these conferences is not explicitly and absolutely forbidden, does it suffice for a Catholic to regulate his conduct according to the principles of the natural law, or is he further bound by ecclesiastical legislation, for example, does he require the permission of his superiors before he may licitly participate in one of these conferences?

Besides the legislation which may be found in the Code, there are several pronouncements of the Holy See regarding the participation of Catholics in these conferences. It has been deemed necessary to consider at length the conferences which occasioned these pronouncements in order that the pronouncements themselves may be properly understood. Moreover, since the pronouncements which have been made since the advent of the Code are more closely allied with the pronouncements which preceded the Code than with the legislation of the Code itself, all of these pronouncements, both those which preceded and those which followed the Code, will be considered before a treatment of the legislation of the Code is undertaken.

CHAPTER V

CONFERENCES BEFORE THE CODE

Article 1. The Association for the Promotion of the Union of Christendom

About the year 1850 a movement was undertaken by a group of Anglicans to bring about a corporate reunion between the Anglican Church and the Church of Rome. Ambrose Phillipps De Lisle (1809-1878), a convert to Catholicism, became zealously interested in the movement, and sent a glowing, perhaps exaggerated, account of it to Cardinal Barnabo, then the Prefect of the Sacred Congregation for the Propagation of the Faith. In a letter to De Lisle the Cardinal voiced his approval,[1] and De Lisle took this as a sign that he was to take an active part in the movement. As a result he met with the Anglicans on July 4, 1857, and sent the resolutions of this meeting to the Cardinal. These resolutions were: first, the vote of a golden chalice to His Eminence as a token of gratitude and as a pledge of the hoped-for reunion between the English and the Roman Churches; second, the foundation of an Association of prayer, for which the Pope was asked to grant an indulgence, which should be, if possible, extended to Anglicans. On September 8 of the same year the articles of the Association for the Promotion of the Union of Christendom were drawn up by F. G. Lee (an Anglican minister) and De Lisle.[2]

---

[1] Perhaps it is this letter to which Slosser (a non-Catholic) refers when he says that the Pope blessed the movement at its inception.—*Christian Unity, Its History and Challenge* (London: Kegan Paul, Trench, Trubner & Co., Ltd., 1929), p. 214.

It is erroneous, however, to draw such a conclusion from this letter since the Association for the Promotion of the Union of Christendom had not yet been founded at the time this letter was written. Moreover, the Cardinal only praised the fact that a number of Anglicans were seeking to be reunited with the Catholic Church. At that time he knew nothing of the errors inherent in the movement.

[2] Except where it is otherwise noted, the historical facts concerning the

The majority of English Catholics opposed the movement and they voiced their disapproval on the following grounds: first, at least the Anglican members of the Association believed in the "branch theory," namely, that the Anglican, Orthodox, and Roman Catholic Churches were equal members of the one Church of Christ; second, the movement fostered a neglect of individual conversions; third, the comparative size of the Anglican bloc and the number of Catholics interested in the movement had been grossly exaggerated. Inasmuch as the members of the movement were wont to misconstrue his notions of corporate union as expressed in a *Letter on Catholic Unity* written to the Earl of Shrewsbury, Cardinal Wiseman (1802-1865) was constrained to make a report to the Sacred Congregation for the Propagation of the Faith making clear his position in the matter.[3]

Cardinal Barnabo, in a letter to De Lisle, refused to accept the chalice which had been offered to him on the grounds that the acceptance of such a gift would seem to imply that the Sacred Congregation, of which he was the president, assented to, or connived at, false doctrine.

The Association, founded in the year 1857, continued to expand until 1864. Membership was offered to adherents of the Roman Catholic, Greek-Schismatic and Anglican communions. Prayers and Masses were to be offered by all members for the intention that these three communions might be united in one. No discussion of religious differences was allowed. Each member was to follow the teachings of his own communion.

Although Catholics were not officially prohibited from becoming members, the attitude of the English hierarchy toward the Association became increasingly hostile with each passing year. This was due to the criticisms already mentioned and to the nature of some

Association for the Promotion of the Union of Christendom have been taken from Thureau-Dangin's *The English Catholic Revival in the Nineteenth Century* (revised and re-edited from a translation by the late Wilfred Wilberforce, 2 vols., London: Simpkin, Marshall, Hamilton, Kent & Co., Ltd., 1914), II, 184-202.

[3] Ward, *Life and Times of Cardinal Wiseman* (2. ed., 2 vols., London: Longmans, Green & Co., 1897), I, 401-406; II, 474-491.

of the articles published in the official organ of the Association, *The Union Review*. This review, besides the fact that it contained questionable doctrines in matters of faith, had become a medium through which certain dissatisfied Catholic priests were able to attack the hierarchy and traditional ecclesiastical legislation.

A variety of causes, then, prompted Cardinal Wiseman and the other English bishops to memorialize the Sacred Congregation for the Propagation of the Faith in 1864 [4] on the participation of Catholics in the Association. The result was a severe letter from the Sacred Congregation condemning this and similar societies.[5]

It is strongly asserted in this letter that true Christian unity is to be prayed for and worked for but

> . . . quod Christifideles et ecclesiastici viri, haereticorum ductu et, quod peius est, iuxta intentionem haeresi quam maxime pollutam et infectam, pro Christiana unitate orent, tolerari nullo modo potest.

The bishops were advised to warn the faithful of the errors and evils which are bound to result from such a society. They are counseled

> . . . ut edoceantur fideles ne haereticorum ductu hanc cum iisdem haereticis et schismaticis societatem ineant. . . . Caveant igitur summo studio Christifideles ne hisce societatibus coniungantur, quibus salva fidei integritate nequeunt adhaerere.

Indifferentism and scandal are shown to be two of the evils which may result, and finally,

> Maxima igitur sollicitudine curandum est, ne Catholici, vel specie pietatis vel mala sententia decepti, Societati, de qua hic

---

[4] Slosser (*op. cit.*, p. 214) states that the scheme was blessed as late as 1863 when one of the English Secretaries was granted an audience by the Pope. This fact is not verified by any official document, nor is it likely, in view of the events which were taking place in England at the time, that the Pope blessed the Association as such. Probably, as in the case of Cardinal Barnabo, he merely approved the fact that a group of Anglicans were seeking to be reunited to the true Church of Christ.

[5] 16 sept. 1864—*AAS*, XI (1919), 310-312. This letter is found only in the *AAS* for the year 1919, when it was republished for the reasons stated in the final chapter.

habitus est sermo, aliisque similibus adscribantur vel quoquo-
modo foveant, et ne, fallaci novae Christianae unitatis desiderio
abrepti, ab ea desciscant unitate perfecta, quae mirabili munere
gratiae Dei in Petri soliditate consistit.

Upon the publication of this letter the Anglican reunionists
wrote a reply to the Holy Office in which they sorrowfully and
respectfully protested that their intentions had been misinterpreted.
They asked Cardinal Wiseman to present this letter to Rome in their
behalf. Before anything could be done, however, Wiseman died
and was succeeded by Manning. The new archbishop permitted
the letter to be presented to the Holy Office, but suggested at the
same time that Rome take a firm stand and put a stop to the whole
affair.[6] This occasioned another letter from the Holy Office, a letter
to certain English Puseyites.[7] This letter was not as ostensibly
severe as the first, but it contained substantially the same message.
The true notion of Catholic unity was expounded and the "branch
theory" was shown to be false. It was explained why Catholics
had been forbidden to participate in societies established for the
promotion of the unity of Christendom as the Puseyites understood
this unity.

These letters sounded the death-knell of the Association. Catholics, including De Lisle, immediately withdrew their membership.
The Association continued in existence for some years after its
condemnation by the Holy Office, but never attained any far-reach-
ing influence.

From a canonical viewpoint there is little to be said concerning
these letters of the Holy Office. In condemning societies (and
therefore meetings and conferences sponsored by these societies)
which are founded for the purpose of uniting all Christians in one

---

[6] Manning (1808-1892) had no sympathy with the movement and very little
for its adherents. He did not agree that their intentions had been misinterpreted. Wiseman, until his attitude changed under Manning's influence, and
Newman, although they did not believe in the movement, did not favor a harsh
condemnation because they respected the good-will and earnest intentions of the
participants, especially the Catholics.

[7] 8 nov. 1865—*AAS*, XI (1919), 312-316. This letter appears only in the
AAS for the year 1919, when it was republished for reasons which will be stated
in the final chapter.

federation without the complete submission of one and all to the Catholic Church in matters of faith and morals, the Sacred Congregation is merely putting into explicit terms a clear precept of the divine natural and positive law. Briefly, the letters prohibit participation in two types of conferences: those which aim at a union of the churches with due allowance for particular differences, that is, on the basis of a lowest common denominator; and those which strive to promote tolerance by imbuing the participants with a respect for the diverse religions of others. It is obvious that these two prohibitions are still in effect.

ARTICLE 2. THE WORLD'S PARLIAMENT OF RELIGIONS

The World's Parliament of Religions, to which delegates from all religions of the world were invited, was held in Chicago in 1893 in connection with the Columbian Exposition. A complete account of the purpose, organization, and proceedings of the Parliament has been edited by a Presbyterian minister, John Henry Barrows, the Chairman of the General Committee on Religious Congresses of the World's Congress Auxiliary.[8]

The objects proposed for the Parliament were as follows:[9]

1. To bring together in conference for the first time in history the leading representatives of the great Historic Religions of the world.

2. To show to men, in the most impressive way, what and how many important truths the various Religions hold in common.

3. To promote and deepen the spirit of human brotherhood among religious men of diverse faiths, through friendly conference and mutual good understanding, while not seeking to foster the temper of indifferentism, and not striving to achieve any outward and formal unity.

4. To set forth, by those most competent to speak, what are deemed the important distinctive truths held and taught by each Religion, and by the various chief branches of Christendom.

5. To indicate the impregnable foundations of Theism, and

---

[8] *The World's Parliament of Religions* (2 vols., Chicago: The Parliament Publishing Co., 1893).

[9] *Op. cit.*, I, 18.

the reasons for man's faith in Immortality, and thus to unite and strengthen the forces which are adverse to a materialistic philosophy of the universe.

6. To secure from leading scholars, representing the Brahman, Buddhist, Confucian, Parsee, Mohammedan, Jewish and other Faiths, and from representatives of the various Churches of Christendom, full and accurate statements of the spiritual and other effects of the Religions which they hold upon the Literature, Art, Commerce, Government, Domestic and Social life of the peoples among whom these Faiths have prevailed.

7. To inquire what light each Religion has afforded, or may afford, to the other Religions of the world.

8. To set forth, for permanent record to be published to the world, an accurate and authoritative account of the present condition and outlook of Religion among the leading nations of the earth.

9. To discover, from competent men, what light Religion has to throw on the great problems of the present age, especially the important questions connected with Temperance, Labor, Education, Wealth and Poverty.

10. To bring the nations of the earth into a more friendly fellowship, in the hope of securing permanent international peace.

The purpose of the Parliament is further elucidated in the Preliminary Address sent out to the world by the General Committee in 1891.[10]

The idea of the World Congress was almost universally approved, yet there were notes of dissent.[11] It is interesting to note that the Archbishop of Canterbury disapproved of the Parliament on the grounds that since the Christian religion is the one true religion it could not become a member of a Parliament of religions, since then it would have to assume the equality of other members and the parity of their positions and claims.[12]

According to Dr. Barrows,

[10] *Op. cit.*, I, 10.

[11] *Op. cit.*, I, 18-26.

In a pamphlet entitled *Search Light, The Testimony of the Bible Versus the Parliament of the Religions* (Des Moines: Iowa Printing Co., 1893) the Rev. A. C. Tris bitterly criticizes the Parliament.

[12] *Op. cit.*, I, 21-22.

. . . the Catholic Archbishops of America, at their meeting in New York in November, 1892, took action approving the participation of the Catholic Church in the Parliament and appointed the Rt. Rev. John J. Keane, the able and liberal-minded Rector of the Catholic University of America in Washington, to arrange with the General Committee for the proper and adequate presentation of the Catholic doctrine on the questions coming before the Parliament.[13]

Several members of the Catholic hierarchy played prominent rôles in the Parliament. Cardinal Gibbons (1834-1921), Archbishop Ireland (1838-1918) of St. Paul (a member of the Advisory Council) and Bishop Keane (1839-1918) wrote letters heartily approving of the Parliament.[14] At the opening session the people were led by the Cardinal in the Lord's Prayer,[15] and were later addressed by him,[16] by Archbishop Feehan (1829-1902) of Chicago (a member of the General Committee)[17] and by Archbishop Redwood (1839-1935) of New Zealand.[18] During the course of the Parliament papers were read by the Cardinal and Bishop Keane.[19]

About two years after the close of the Parliament, on September 18, 1895, in a letter to the then Apostolic Delegate to the United States, later Cardinal Satolli (1839-1910), Leo XIII temperately discountenanced participation by Catholics in such promiscuous religious meetings.[20]

Coetus in foederatis Americae civitatibus celebrari subinde novimus in quos viri promiscue conveniant tum e catholico nomine, tum ex iis qui a catholica ecclesia dissident, simul de religione rectisque moribus acturi. In hoc quidem studium agnoscimus religiosae rei, quo gens ista ardentius in dies fertur. At quamvis communes hi coetus ad hunc diem prudenti silentio tolerati sunt, consultius tamen videatur si catholici homines suos seorsum conventus agant: quorum tamen utilitas ne in ipso unice derivetur, ea lege indici poterunt, ut aditus audiendum universis patent, iis etiam qui ab Ecclesia catholica seiunguntur.

[13] *Op. cit.*, I, 15.
[14] *Op. cit.*, I, 14, 16-17.
[15] *Op. cit.*, I, 67.
[16] *Op. cit.*, I, 80-81.
[17] *Op. cit.*, I, 79-80.
[18] *Op. cit.*, I, 94-95.
[19] *Op. cit.*, I, 485-493; II, 882-888, 1032-1036, 1331-1338.
[20] *SS. D. N. Leonis XIII Acta* (6 vols., Brugis et Insulis, 1887-1900), VI, 97.

This letter, in the light of the history of the World's Parliament of Religions, appears to be directed against that type of meeting between Catholics and non-Catholics in which a real and immediate danger of indifferentism is present. Such a meeting differs specifically from conferences which aim at union on the basis of a lowest common denominator or which strive directly to imbue their participants with a respect for the diverse religions of others. If this were not the case, Leo XIII would not have couched his reproof in such mild terms. Moreover, the character of the Catholic participants must be taken into consideration. Until the opposite is proved, it may be presumed that men of their moral and intellectual qualities would not have heartily approved, even unconsciously, of a movement which was intrinsically evil.

Discussions on religion and morality between Catholics and non-Catholics are not forbidden in themselves, since it is suggested that they may be held under Catholic auspices. This fact lends weight to the conclusion that these discussions are not always intrinsically evil (as was decided in the case of the Association for the Promotion of the Union of Christendom), but are sometimes to be judged as licit or illicit according to their extrinsic circumstances. Where the circumstances are such (as was decided in the case of the World's Parliament of Religions) that a real and immediate danger of indifferentism is present because of the fact that the different religions, as such, seem to be placed on a basis of equality, Catholic participation is necessarily forbidden.

CHAPTER VI

CONFERENCES AFTER THE CODE

ARTICLE 1. UNION-OF-THE-CHURCH MEETINGS

BEGINNING in 1910, the Episcopal Church in the United States sponsored a World Conference on Faith and Order. The invitation to participate was extended to all churches which accepted the fact and doctrine of the Incarnation. The purpose of the society was explained in a Latin pamphlet entitled *De unione ecclesiarum ac totius Christianitatis societatis congressu pro quaestionibus ad fidem ordinemque ecclesiae spectantibus rite explorandis ac perpendendis.* Participation was to involve no surrender or compromise of any doctrine or position held by any Church. Disagreements were to be studied and discussed not controversially, but in an effort for mutual understanding and appreciation.

The secretary of this conference, in a letter to Cardinal Gasparri (1852-1934), asked the prayers of the Holy Father for its success, and received a gracious reply.[1] In May, 1919, delegates from the Conference called upon the Holy Father. Although they were kindly received, the delegates were informed that neither representatives of the Pope nor other Catholic men could take part in the meetings of the Conference precisely because it was not based on a unity of faith and of rule.[2]

More than likely this Conference was the occasion for the Holy Office being asked, on July 4, 1919, "whether the instructions of this Supreme Sacred Congregation, of September 16, 1864, regarding the participation of Catholics in a certain society founded in London to procure the unity of Christendom are to be applied and obeyed by the faithful also in regard to their participation in meetings or conferences of whatever kind, public or private, called by non-

---

[1] *AAS,* IX (1917), 61.

[2] *Periodica,* X (1922), 34; Bouscaren, *The Canon Law Digest* (2 vols. and a supplement, Milwaukee: Bruce, 1934-1941), I, 621.

Catholics for the purpose of promoting the union of all churches claiming to be Christian." The reply was in the affirmative, and the letters of September 16, 1864, and September 8, 1865, were ordered to be republished in the *Acta Apostolicae Sedis.*[3]

In the year 1925 the Lutheran Archbishop of Sweden, Doctor Nathan Soderblom (1866-1931), convoked a general assembly of all the Christian Churches to be held in Stockholm, August 19-30, 1925.[4] In contrast to the World Conference on Faith and Order, this assembly was to omit entirely all discussion of dogmatic questions. It was to deal with Christianity insofar as it established principles of morality in the domestic, social, political and international spheres.

Desirous of obtaining the approval of the Holy Father, the moderators of this assembly sent a representative to the Vatican to ask Pius XI if he would appoint a pontifical delegate to the Conference. The visitor was received courteously and kindly by the Holy Father, but no papal representative appeared in Stockholm.

Rome spoke again on the question of union-of-the-church meetings when, on the occasion of a conference held at Lausanne in Switzerland, August 3-21, 1927, the Holy Office was asked "whether Catholics are allowed to belong to or to favor conventions, meetings, conferences, or associations of non-Catholics which have for their purpose to unite all those who call themselves Christians in one religious federation."[5] The reply was in the negative and the Holy Office stated that its decree of July 4, 1919, regarding the participation of Catholics in the society "for the Union of Christendom" was absolutely to be observed.[6]

On January 10, 1928, Pius XI, in an encyclical letter, *"Mortalium animos,"*[7] confirmed the resolutions of the Holy Office of 1864,

[3] *AAS*, XI (1919), 309. The two letters in chronological order are reprinted in connection with this decree. Cf. *AAS*, XI (1919), 310-312 and 312-316.

[4] Dudon, "La Conférence Chrétienne de Stockholm," *Etudes*, CLXXXV (1925), 641-657.

[5] S. C. S. Off., Dubium *de conventibus (quas dicunt) ad procurandam omnium Christianorum unitatem*, 8 iul. 1927.

[6] *AAS*, XIX (1927), 278.

[7] *AAS*, XX (1928), 5-16.

1865, 1919 and 1927 by absolutely forbidding Catholics to participate in conferences which have for their purpose to unite all those who call themselves Christians in one religious federation. This letter is especially noteworthy for its clear diagnosis of the errors inherent in all attempts at a union of the various Christian Churches through compromise or syncretism of doctrine. It is pointed out that true Christian unity is a unity of faith and rule which can be had on this earth only through the incorporation of all men into the Mystical Body of Christ, the Catholic Church.

This letter did not add anything new to the already existing ecclesiastical regulations concerning the participation of Catholics in doctrinal discussions with non-Catholics. The principles enunciated in it, though they are clearly and strikingly presented, are as old as the Church.

ARTICLE 2. THE MALINES CONVERSATIONS

During the years 1921-1926 a series of five conferences on matters of faith—the so-called "Malines Conversations"—took place under the sponsorship of prominent members of the Catholic and Anglican Churches.[8] The leading figure for the Anglicans was Lord Halifax;[9] for the Catholics, Cardinal Mercier (1851-1926), the Archbishop of Malines in Belgium. The Conversations were of a strictly private nature, carried on within a select closed group in a private home.[10] It was only some time after the close of the

----

[8] December 6, 7, 1921; March 14, 15, 1923; November 7, 9, 1923; May 20, 1925; October 11, 1926.

[9] Lord Halifax published four pamphlets during the course of the Conversations: *A Call to Reunion, Further Considerations on Behalf of Reunion, Catholic Reunion, Notes on the Conversations at Malines* (London: A. R. Mowbray & Co., Ltd., 1922, 1923, 1926, 1928).

[10] "Celles-ci, de la première a la dernière, furent privées: c'etaient des *conversations* dans un salon privé. . . .

"Nos rencontres furent donc des conversations privées; elles n'engageaient que notre responsabilité personelle."—Mercier, *Les "Conversations de Malines,"* Lettre a son clerge, le 18 janvier 1924. The original of this letter is found in *Documents on Christian Unity, 1920-1924* (edited by George Kennedy Allen Bell, London: Oxford University Press, 1924), pp. 349-365. An English translation is found in Frere's *Recollections of Malines* (London: Centenary Press, 1935), pp. 90-109.

Conversations, contrary to the wishes of the Catholic authorities, that their proceedings were published by Lord Halifax.[11]

The opinion of Vermeersch (1858-1936)[12] and Bouscaren,[13] that these conferences were not meant to effect or to pave the way for a union of the Anglican with the Catholic Church, but merely to make the way of conversion easier for individuals, does not seem to agree with the facts in the case. The literature on the subject, including statements made by Cardinal Mercier and Lord Halifax, points conclusively to the fact that the ultimate purpose of the Conversations was to pave the way for union.[14] Such an idea seems in itself very laudable, since it can safely be presumed that Cardinal Mercier would only have sought a union of the Churches in the true Catholic sense.

The Cardinal presided at the first four conferences, and after his death, the new archbishop, Van Roey, who had assisted at the previous Conversations as the Cardinal's vicar general, presided at the fifth. On January 25, 1928, approximately a year and a half after the last Conversation, Van Roey made it clear that he did not see any possibility of continuing the Conversations.[15] Just a few days previous to this, on January 21, 1928, the *Osservatore Romano* had carried this announcement: "We can say again with absolute assurance that the resumption of the Conversations would certainly not have the consent or encouragement of the Holy Father." It was further stated that the Conversations had been a strictly private venture undertaken without any mandate from the Holy See.

[11] *The Conversations at Malines* (London: Oxford University Press, 1927 [French and English edition], 1930 [English edition]).

[12] *Periodica*, XVII (1928), 13.

[13] "Cooperation with Non-Catholics, Canonical Legislation," *Theological Studies*, III (1942), 508.

[14] Goyau, *Cardinal Mercier* (London: Longmans, Green & Co., Ltd., 1926), Preface, pp. VIII-XVIII; Laveille, *A Life of Cardinal Mercier* (translated by Arthur Livingstone, New York: The Century Co., 1928), pp. 212-217; Dubly, *The Life of Cardinal Mercier, Primate of Belgium* (translated from the French by Herbert Wilson, London: Sands & Co., 1928), pp. 235-255. The contents, and even the very titles, of the pamphlets published by Lord Halifax furnish further proof of the above stated fact. Cf. note 8 of this Chapter.

[15] Bolton, *A Catholic Memorial of Lord Halifax and Cardinal Mercier* (London: Williams & Norgate, Ltd., 1935), p. 142.

While it is certain that Rome never officially approved of the Conversations and actually frowned upon them *post factum*, it nevertheless seems logical to conjecture with Vermeersch [16] that Cardinal Mercier would never have favored the undertaking unless it had been at least tacitly permitted by the Holy See. No other conclusion is possible if one is to believe the Cardinal when he writes that his efforts have been blessed and encouraged by the Holy See although he has not acted as her official representative.[17] Bishop Frere, one of the non-Catholic participants, states that Cardinal Mercier kept Rome informed concerning the Conversations. He reports that after the first Conversation the Cardinal wrote that he had reason to believe that the Conversations were being followed with approval in Rome and that their continuance would be well-regarded. He further states that after the second Conversation the Cardinal reported to Rome on the subject of the Conversations and received a very encouraging reply.[18]

From a canonical point of view there is little to be said concerning these Conversations. Certainly the official sanction of the Holy See would have been necessary if the Conversations had been directed toward an immediate union of the Churches. Such was not the case, however. The entire movement was merely an attempt on the part of private individuals to remove some of the obstacles which blocked the road to union. The idea seems to have been good in itself, but it was the judgment of the Holy See that it did not work out in practice. Whether this judgment was motivated by extrinsic circumstances, by the erroneous notions of some of the participants, or by other causes, it is difficult to say.

It may be significant that the statements of Van Roey and the *Osservatore Romano* came out within a fortnight after Pius XI published his encyclical letter on Christian Unity. Vermeersch seems

[16] *Periodica*, XVII (1928), 13.

[17] "Nos échanges d'idées ne furent donc pas des 'négociations.' Pour negocier, il faut être porteur d'un mandat et, ni de part ni d'autre, nous n'avions de mandat. Aussi bien, en ce qui nous concerne, n'en avions-nous pas sollicité: il nous suffisait de savoir que nous marchions d'accord avec l'Autorité supreme, bénis et encouragés par Elle."—*Les "Conversations de Malines"—Documents on Christian Unity, 1920-1924*, p. 353.

[18] *Recollections of Malines*, pp. 31, 35.

to look upon this sequence of events as purely coincidental.[19]   Certainly it would be difficult to prove that these statements which brought an end to the Conversations were *post hoc ergo propter hoc,* especially since there were other movements afoot at the time against which the encyclical letter was obviously directed.

[19] *Periodica,* XVII (1928), 13.

CHAPTER VII

THE LEGISLATION OF THE CODE

Canon 1325, § 3. Caveant catholici ne disputationes vel collationes, publicas praesertim, cum acatholicis habeant, sine venia Sanctae Sedis aut, si casus urgeat, loci Ordinarii.

ARTICLE 1. THE RELATION BETWEEN THE PRONOUNCEMENTS OF THE HOLY SEE AND CANON 1325, § 3

THE pronouncements of the Holy See discussed in the two previous Chapters simply state in explicit terms regulations which flow from the natural law and from the constitutional law of the Church. The principles expressed in these pronouncements do not bring into being any purely ecclesiastical legislation. They were in force before the pronouncements were made and they are still in force today. At the time of their publication these pronouncements were important because they put a stop to movements which in the mind of the Holy See constituted serious threats to the preservation and extension of the true faith of Christ. They are important today because they serve to keep the faithful on guard against the errors denounced in them, errors which are still prevalent in the modern world.

In these pronouncements are affirmed the general prohibitions whereby participation in certain types of discussions with non-Catholics are forbidden to all Catholics. It is important to notice, however, that the decision as to whether or not any particular discussion, other than those expressly mentioned, falls under these prohibitions is left (if one prescinds from the necessity of a canonical mission) to the judgment of the individual Catholics concerned.

If it is maintained that discussions other than formal disputations on matters of faith with non-Catholics are comprehended within the object of canon 1325, § 3, then it follows that a new regulation, one not contained in the pronouncements of the Holy See, is brought into being, for in such a hypothesis the decision as to the lawfulness or unlawfulness of every particular such discussion would be reserved to the Holy See or, in urgent cases, to the local ordinary.

ARTICLE 2. THE FORCE OF CANON 1325, § 3

The purpose of this article is to decide whether or not formal discussions between Catholics and non-Catholics other than oral debates are affected by the legislation of the canon 1325, § 3. This decision will rest entirely upon the signification of the words, *"disputationes vel collationes."*

There are reasons for maintaining that the two words denote one and the same thing, namely, disputations strictly so-called, or, in other words, prearranged, oral, formal debates.[1] First of all, in the footnotes of his edition of the Code, Cardinal Gasparri cites only decrees which treat of disputations.[2] Moreover, in these documents the words *"colloquia," "disputationes," "collationes," "conferentiae"* and *"congressus"* are used interchangeably to signify discussions of an argumentative character, disputations strictly so-called. In commenting on the text most of the authors state that the law comprehends only formal disputations.[3] These authors discuss the morality of meetings other than formal disputations, but they do not consider such meetings as comprehended by the law of canon

---

[1] The proponents of this opinion assert that canon 1325, § 3, is but a restatement of the old law concerning discussions with non-Catholics as found in the decrees of the Sacred Congregation for the Propagation of the Faith and the Holy Office. These decrees treat only of disputations. This is evident from the general tenor of the decrees themselves and from the historical events which were taking place at the time of their promulgation.

[2] *Fontes*, nn. 4428, 4457, 4467. For the text of these decrees see footnotes 19, 20, 21, of Chapter III. Cf. pp. 26-27.

[3] Ayrinhac, *Administrative Legislation*, n. 165; De Meester, *Compendium*, n. 1284; Coronata, *Institutiones*, n. 912; Wernz-Vidal, *Ius Canonicum*, Tom. IV, n. 619; Vermeersch, *Theologiae Moralis Principia*, Tom. II, n. 52; Beste, *Introductio in Codicem* (Collegeville: St. John's Abbey Press, 1938), p. 646; Genicot, *Institutiones Theologiae Moralis* (ed. 10 [3 post Codicem Iuris Canonici] quam recognovit I. Salsman, 2 vols., Bruxellis: Alb. Dewit, 1922), I, n. 201.

1325, § 3. Finally, though since 1918 conferences on religious matters (as opposed to disputations) have been more numerous than formal disputations, no official statement has been made as to the bearing of canon 1325, § 3, on these conferences, nor have their critics attacked them on the grounds that they could not be entered into without the permission required by this canon.

There are those, however, who maintain that the words *"disputationes"* and *"collationes"* denote truly different ideas. According to their interpretation *"collatio"* designates any formal discussion between Catholics and non-Catholics on matters of faith other than a formal disputation,[4] *e. g.*, union-of-the-church meetings, round-table discussions, parliaments of religion, etc. A number of arguments can be brought forth in favor of this opinion. First, the words *"disputationes"* and *"collationes"* in their ordinary usage denote two distinctly different ideas. Secondly, if only formal disputations are the object of the law, it was a useless and unnecessary gesture to employ the two words. Thirdly, the particle *"vel"* is sufficiently strong to be considered as truly disjunctive. The particle *"aut"* is not used because, although the ideas expressed by the two words are different, they are not contradictory, nor are they opposed to each other in the text of the law.

Although the arguments in favor of this latter opinion may suf-

---

[4] "These words include both disputations or debates, and friendly meetings or conferences which aim at agreement or accord."—Bouscaren, "Cooperation with Non-Catholics, Canonical Legislation," *Theological Studies*, III (1942), 504.

"Besides debates, the canon forbids conferences—apparently that type of meeting in which the representative of each denomination propounds and explains his creed without directly aiming at a refutation of the others."—Connell, "Catholics and 'Interfaith' Groups," *The Ecclesiastical Review*, CV (1942), 342.

"These conferences include round-table discussions, union-of-the-church meetings, open forums, public debates."—McVann, *The Canon Law on Sermon Preaching* (New York: The Paulist Press, 1940), p. 157.

". . . conferences—including the so-called parliaments of religion. . . ."—Augustine, *A Commentary on the New Code of Canon Law* (8 vols., Vol. VI, 3. ed., St. Louis: B. Herder Book Co., 1931), VI, 335.

"Addit vero canon: vel collationes, tanquam amicabilia colloquia."—Blat, *Commentarium*, Lib. III[2], n. 199.

fice to make it intrinsically probable,[5] the former opinion—according to which only formal disputations are affected by the law—seems to be the more tenable one. It fits in more harmoniously with the history of the question up to 1918, and since it, too, is certainly probable, both intrinsically and extrinsically,[6] it is to be preferred to the latter opinion because of the provision of canon 6, 4°.[7] Moreover, once the probability of the former opinion is admitted, the latter opinion is excluded by virtue of canon 15.[8]

It may, perhaps, be argued that disputations belong to the dim historic past, and that the problem which confronts the Church in the twentieth century concerns conferences and meetings other than disputations. The truth of this assertion is readily granted, but while it may be used as an argument to show that the present law is outmoded or incomplete, yet it cannot be used to interpret the law as dealing equally with this modern problem without doing violence to the accepted rules of interpretation.

Since the conclusion that the object of the law is restricted to disputations strictly so-called has been accepted only *salvo meliori iudicio*, it will not be out of place to discuss the type of conference which would be forbidden if the word *"collationes"* did refer to meetings other than disputations.

Granted that the word *"collationes"* denotes conferences or meetings as opposed to disputations strictly so-called, the next question is, to what type, or types, of conferences does the law refer? If one were to consider the text simply as it stands, then it would follow that each and every public conference between Catholics and non-Catholics is comprehended, regardless of its end, object, or circum-

---

[5] These arguments, based on an abstract consideration of the words *"disputationes"* and *"collationes,"* lose a great deal of their force when these words are considered in the light of their past canonical usage.

[6] Bouscaren and Augustine are the only two authors who in treating the subject *ex professo* explicitly favor the latter opinion.

[7] "In dubio num aliquod canonum praescriptum cum veteri iure discrepet, a veteri iure non est recendendum."

[8] "Leges, etiam irritantes et inhabilitantes, in dubio iuris non urgent;—" It is not maintained that canon 1325, § 3, is a *lex irritans* or a *lex inhabilitans*. Although *leges irritantes* and *leges inhabilitantes* are pointed to with special emphasis in canon 15, it is clear that the canon refers to *all* laws.

stances. For example, to give an extreme case, a public discussion on the merits of transportation by air would be comprehended by the law.

However, the words of ecclesiastical laws are to be understood according to their proper signification as considered in the *text and context*.[9] Therefore, since this entire part of the Code is concerned with the ecclesiastical *magisterium*, it must be concluded that only those conferences are comprehended by the law in which matters of faith are discussed.[10]

It has been said of formal disputations that they are in themselves licit. The morality of any particular formal disputation is to be determined by a consideration of its circumstances. Can the same thing be said of conferences on matters of faith? Are they, all of them, in themselves licit? The answer is decidedly in the negative. Conferences (1) which aim at union on the basis of a lowest common denominator, or (2) which try to imbue their participants with a respect for the diverse religious beliefs of others, can never be licit. They may be said to be on a par with dubitative disputations inasmuch as they are absolutely forbidden at all times regardless of circumstances.

On the other hand, it is possible to envisage (3) a formal discussion between Catholics and non-Catholics from which the above ends have been excluded and in which the primary purpose is to foster personal tolerance, or better still, a spirit of Christian charity. Granted that the ends of such conferences are good, their morality will be determined by a consideration of the circumstances in each particular case. This same conclusion will be true with regard to conferences (4) in which the immediate purpose is to bring one or more non-Catholics into the true Church of Christ, or (5) in which the participants are concerned with moral, social, or civic issues. As regards this last type of conference, it must be remembered that it is comprehended within the law only when it includes discussions on matters of faith.

If all and only such conferences as described above are comprehended by canon 1325, § 3, then the object and purpose of the

[9] Canon 18.
[10] Cf. *supra*, p. 32.

law may be summed up as follows: since it is frequently difficult
to decide to which of the five types a particular conference belongs,
and since it is still more difficult, once it is granted that the conference in question is not to be classed among the first two groups,
to decide whether or not the circumstances are of such a nature as
to give rise to a well-founded hope that the conference will be beneficial to the Church, the Holy See has reserved to itself the decision
as to the lawfulness or unlawfulness of participating in these conferences in every case.

In this hypothesis the entire law would read as follows: all
Catholics, including Orientals, are forbidden to participate in prearranged formal discussions on matters of faith with heretics, schismatics, apostates, Jews or infidels unless they have previously received permission to do so from the Holy Office or, in urgent cases,
from the ordinary of the place where the discussion is to be held.
The law ceases to bind if, in a given case, even the ordinary of the
place cannot be reached.[11]

ARTICLE 3. THE NECESSITY OF A CANONICAL MISSION

As has been stated above, the opinion according to which only
formal disputations strictly so-called are affected by canon 1325, § 3,
seems to present the more tenable interpretation. With the acceptance of this opinion, another question arises. Is Catholic participation in these conferences conditioned upon purely ecclesiastical regulations, or is the lawful or unlawful character of it to be determined
solely according to the principles of the natural law?

In the discussion concerning disputations it was stated and explained at some length that no Catholic may undertake a public
exposition or defense of the truths of faith unless he has first received a canonical mission from the local ordinary or from the
Holy See.[12] This same provision seems to apply here with the result
that no Catholic may participate in a public conference or meeting
in which matters of faith are discussed unless he has the permis-

---

[11] For a complete treatment of the points mentioned in this paragraph cf.
supra, pp. 31-43, where they are considered at length in the discussion of disputations.

[12] Cf. *supra*, pp. 39-40.

sion of at least the local ordinary. The final decision, therefore, as
to the lawful or unlawful character of these conferences lies with
the local ordinary, who is to be guided in his judgment by the principles of the natural law and the norms enacted by the Holy See.
If it should be maintained that the right to participate in these
conferences is contained in the canonical mission to preach,[13] still
the ordinary may very easily, and licitly, restrict this right, for even
a pastor, who obtains a canonical mission to preach by reason of his
office, can only *per se*, exercise this prerogative at stated times and
under certain specified conditions.[14]

Finally, if it is the prudent judgment of the ordinary that certain types of discussions or conferences with non-Catholics, no
matter what the nature of the subject-matter or circumstances be,
constitute a danger to the faith or morals of his subjects, he can
legislate as he sees fit concerning Catholic participation in these
conferences.[15]

By analogy with canon 1397, § 5, which treats of the prohibition
of books,[16] it can be seen that cases could arise wherein the local
ordinary would be obliged to seek a pronouncement from the Holy
See. These are: first, if the issues involved in a particular conference are of so subtle a nature that they merit the consideration of
the supreme authority; secondly, if the local ordinary prudently
foresees that his prohibition against participation in a particular
conference may be disregarded unless it is supported by the Holy
See; thirdly, if a particular conference deserving of condemnation
constitutes a problem in more than one diocese and it is prudently
foreseen that even the joint or common action of the ordinaries of
the dioceses involved may not be sufficient to bring about an effective
condemnation.

13 Canons 1337-1348.

14 Canon 1344.

15 Canon 336, § 2.

16 "Libros qui subtilius examen exigant vel de quibus ad salutarem effectum
consequendum supremae auctoritatis sententia requiri videatur, ad Apostolicae
Sedis iudicium Ordinarii deferant."

CONCLUSIONS AND SUMMARY

IN the following paragraphs the word "conference" will be used
to designate any discussion on matters of faith between Catholics
and non-Catholics other than a formal disputation.

1. The pronouncements made by the Holy See concerning these
conferences are simply explicit declarations of provisions which flow
from the natural law and from the constitutional law of the Church.

2. The principles contained in these pronouncements are as old
as the Church itself. They contain no purely ecclesiastical regulations. They were in effect before the pronouncements themselves
were made, and they are still in effect today.

3. According to these pronouncements, Catholics are forbidden
to participate in certain types of conferences with non-Catholics.
The decision as to whether or not this or that particular conference
falls under the prohibition is left (if one prescinds from the necessity of a canonical mission) to the judgment of the individual Catholics concerned.

4. If it is maintained that these conferences are comprehended
within the object of canon 1325, § 3, then it follows that a new
regulation, one not contained in the pronouncements of the Holy
See, is brought into being, for in such an hypothesis the decision as
to the lawfulness or unlawfulness of every particular conference
would be reserved to the Holy See or, in urgent cases, to the local
ordinary.

5. Although it is conceded that the opinion according to which
these conferences are comprehended within the object of canon 1325,
§ 3, is intrinsically probable, nevertheless it is maintained that the
opinion according to which the words *"disputationes vel collationes"*
refer only to disputations strictly so-called, since it too is intrinsically probable, is to be accepted in virtue of canon 6, 4° and canon 15.

6. With the acceptance of this opinion it follows that the decision as to lawfulness or unlawfulness of particular conferences need
not be sought from the Holy See. This decision, in ordinary cases,
lies with the local ordinary, who alone (with the exception of the

Supreme Pontiff) can grant the required canonical mission without which a Catholic is forbidden to publicly explain or defend the truths of faith.

7. Since it is the office of the local ordinary to safeguard the faith and morals of his subjects, all discussions between Catholics and non-Catholics, no matter what the topic or circumstances, are subject to his supervision.

o

BIBLIOGRAPHY

SOURCES

Acta Apostolicae Sedis, Commentarium Officiale, Romae, 1909—

Acta et Decreta Concilii Plenarii Americae Latinae in Urbe Celebrati, A. D. MDCCCXCIX, Romae: Typis Vaticanis, 1902.

Acta et Decreta Concilii Plenarii Quebecencis Primi Anno Domini MCMIX, Quebeci: typis "L'action Sociale Limitée," 1912.

Acta et Decreta Sacrorum Conciliorum Recentiorum, Collectio Lacensis, 7 vols., Friburgi Brisgoviae, 1870-1890.

Bouscaren, T. Lincoln, *The Canon Law Digest*, 2 vols., and a supplement, Milwaukee: Bruce, 1934-1941.

Bullarum Diplomatum et Privilegiorum Sanctorum Romanorum Pontificum Taurinensis Editio, 24 vols. et Appendix, Augustae Taurinorum, 1857-1872.

Codex Iuris Canonici Pii X Pontificis Maximi iussu digestus Benedicti Papae XV auctoritate promulgatus, Romae: Typis Polyglottis Vaticanis, 1917 (Reimpressio, 1934).

Codex Iustinianus, recognovit et retractavit P. Krueger, Berolini: apud Weidmannos, 1928-1929.

Codex Theodosianus, ed. P. Krueger, Th. Mommsen, P. M. Meyer, 3 vols., Berolini, 1905.

Codicis Iuris Canonici Fontes cura Emi. Petri Card. Gasparri Editi, 9 vols., Romae (postea Civitate Vaticana): Typis Polyglottis Vaticanis, 1923-1939 (Vols. VII-IX *ed. cura et studio Emi. Iustiniani Card. Serēdi*).

Corpus Iuris Canonici, ed. Lipsiensis secunda, instruxit Aemilius Friedberg, 2 vols., Lipsiae, 1879-1881.

Decretum Gratiani emendatum et notationibus illustratum una cum glossis, Romae, 1582.

Gothofredus, Jacobus, *Codex Theodosianus cum Perpetuis Commentariis*, 6 vols. in 7, Lipsiae, 1743.

Liber Sextus Decretalium una cum Clementinis et Extravagantibus Earumque Glossis Restitutis, Romae, 1582.

Mansi, J. D., *Sacrorum Conciliorum Nova et Amplissima Collectio*, 53 vols. in 60, Parisiis, 1901-1927.

Migne, Jacques Paul, *Patrologiae Cursus Completus, Series Graeca*, 161 vols., Parisiis, 1856-1866.

———, *Patrologiae Cursus Completus, Series Latina*, 221 vols., Parisiis, 1844-1864.

SS. D. N. Leonis XIII Acta, 6 vols., Brugis et Insulis, 1887-1900.

AUTHORS

Alzog, John, *Manual of Universal Church History*, translated, with additions, from the ninth and last German edition by F. J. Pabisch and Thos. S. Byrne, 3 vols., Cincinnati: Robert Clarke & Co., 1878.

Ayrinhac, H. A., *Administrative Legislation in the New Code of Canon Law*, New York: Longmans, Green & Co., 1930.

[Bachofen], Charles Augustine, *A Commentary on the New Code of Canon Law*, 8 vols., Vol. VI, 3. ed., St. Louis: B. Herder Book Co., 1931.

Barbosa, Augustinus, *Collectanea doctorum tam veterum quam recentiorum in jus pontificium universum*, 6 vols. in 3, Lugduni, 1716.

————, *Collectanea ex doctoribus tum priscis, tum neotericis in Codicem Justiniani*, 2 vols., Lugduni, 1657.

Barrows, John Henry, *The World's Parliament of Religions*, 2 vols., Chicago: The Parliament Publishing Company, 1893.

Beste, Udalricus, *Introductio in Codicem*, Collegeville: St. John's Abbey Press, 1938.

Billington, Ray Allen, *The Protestant Crusade, 1800-1860*, New York: The Macmillan Company, 1938.

Blat, Albertus, *Commentarium Textus Codicis Iuris Canonici*, 6 vols., Romae: ex Typographia Pontificis in Instituto Pii IX, 1921-1927.

Bolton, Charles Anselm, *A Catholic Memorial of Lord Halifax and Cardinal Mercier*, London: Williams & Norgate, Ltd., 1935.

Brunneman, Johannes, *Commentarius in Codicem Justinianeum*, 2 vols., Coloniae Allobrogum, 1771.

Bucceroni, Ianuarius, *Enchiridion Morale*, 4. ed., Romae, 1905.

Burton, Harold, *The Life of St. Francis de Sales*, adapted from the Abbé Hamon's *Vie de S. Francois de Sales*, 2 vols., London: Burns, Oates & Washbourne, Ltd., 1925.

Coronata, Matthaeus Conte a, *Institutiones Iuris Canonici*, 5 vols. (Vols. I et II, 2. ed.), Taurini: Marietti, 1933-1939.

Dandinus, Anselmus, *De Suspectis de Haeresi*, Romae, 1703.

Delbene, Thomas, *De Officio S. Inquisitionis*, 2 vols., Lugduni, 1666.

De Meester, A., *Juris Canonici et Juris Canonico-Civilis Compendium*, nova editio, ad normam codicis juris canonici, 3 vols. in 4, Brugis: Desclée de Brouwer et Socii, 1921-1928.

Dubly, Henry Louis, *The Life of Cardinal Mercier, Primate of Belgium*, translated from the French by Herbert Wilson, London: Sands & Co., 1928.

Farinacius, Prosper, *Variarum Quaestionum et Communium Opinionum Criminalium, Liber V, de haeresi*, Romae, 1616.

Ferraris, Lucius, *Bibliotheca Canonica, Juridica, Moralis, Theologica, nec non Ascetica, Polemica, Rubricistica, Historica*, 9 vols., Romae, 1885-1899.

Frere, Walter Howard, *Recollections of Malines*, London: Centenary Press, 1935.

Gallizia, Pier Giacinto, *The Life of St. Francis de Sales, Bishop and Prince of Geneva*, translated from the Italian, London, 1854.

Genicot, Eduardus, *Institutiones Theologiae Moralis*, ed. 10, 3. post Codicem Iuris Canonici, quam recognovit I. Salsman, 2 vols., Bruxellis: Alb. Dewit, 1922.

Gonzalez-Tellez, Emmanuel, *Commentaria Perpetua in Singulos Textus Quinque Librorum Decretalium Gregorii IX*, 5 vols. in 4, Venetiis, 1699.

Goyau, Georges, *Cardinal Mercier*, London: Longmans, Green & Co., Ltd., 1926.

Grisar, Hartmann, *Martin Luther, His Life and Work*, adapted from the second German edition by Frank J. Eble, edited by Arthur Preuss, St. Louis: B. Herder, 1930.

Halifax, Viscount Lord, *A Call to Reunion*, London: A. R. Mowbray & Co., Ltd., 1922.

————, *Further Considerations on Behalf of Reunion*, London: A. R. Mowbray & Co., Ltd., 1923.

————, *Catholic Reunion*, London: A. R. Mowbray & Co., Ltd., 1926.

————, *Notes on the Conversations at Malines*, London: A. R. Mowbray & Co., Ltd., 1928.

————, *The Conversations at Malines*, London: Oxford University Press, 1927 (French and English edition); 1930 (English edition).

Hughes, John-Breckinridge, John B., *A Discussion on the Question, "Is the Roman Catholic Religion, in any or in all of its Principles or Doctrines, Inimical to Civil or Religious Liberty?" and the Question, "Is the Presbyterian Religion, in any or in all of its Principles or Doctrines, Inimical to Civil or Religious Liberty?"* Baltimore: John Murphy & Co., c. 1836.

Hughes, Philip, *A History of the Church*, 2 vols., New York: Sheed & Ward, 1935.

Jaffé, Philippus, *Regesta Pontificum Romanorum ab condita Ecclesia ad annum post Christum natum MCXCVIII*, 2. ed. cura Wattenbach, Loewenfeld, Kaltenbrunner, Ewald, 2 vols. in 1, Lipsiae, 1885-1888.

Knabenbauer, Joseph, *Commentarius in Actus Apostolorum*, Parisiis, 1899.

Laveille, A., *A Life of Cardinal Mercier*, translated by Arthur Livingstone, New York: The Century Co., 1928.

McGuire, Thomas-Gregg, T. D., *Authenticated Report of the Discussion between the Rev. T. D. Gregg and the Rev. Thomas McGuire*, Dublin: Richard Coyne, 1839.

McGuire, Thomas-Pope, T. P., *Authenticated report of the discussion which took place between the Rev. Richard T. P. Pope and the Rev. Thomas McGuire in the lecture room of the Dublin Institution, on the 19, 20, 21, 23, 24, 25, of April, 1827*, Dublin, 1827.

McVann, James, *The Canon Law on Sermon Preaching*, New York: The Paulist Press, 1940.

Mercier, Desire Joseph, *Les "Conversations de Malines,"* lettre a son clerge, le 18 janvier 1924—*Documents on Christian Unity, 1920-1924*, edited by George Kennedy Allen Bell, London: Oxford University Press, 1924 (French original); Frere, Walter Howard, *Recollections of Malines*, London: Centenary Press, 1935 (English translation).

Migne, Jacques Paul, *Theologiae Cursus Completus*, 28 vols., Parisiis, 1858-1860, Vol. VI, *De Praeceptis Fidei et de Vitiis Fidei Oppositis*, auctore P. Patuzzi.

Naghten, J. B.-Blakeney, Richard P., *Discussion at Worksop between the Rev. Richard P. Blakeney and the Rev. J. B. Naghten, O.M.I., held in the Music Hall, Worksop, on the evenings of Jan. 30, 31, and Feb. 1, 1850*, reported verbatim by Thomas Whitehead, London, 1850.

Petra, Vincentius, *Commentaria ad Constitutiones Apostolicas*, 5 vols. in 2, Venetiis, 1729.

Petrus Sarnensis, *Petri Vallium Sarnaii Monachi Hystoria Albigensis*, publiée pour la Société de l'histoire de France par Pascal Guébin et Ernest Lyon, 2 tomes, Paris: Librairie Ancienne Honoré Champion, 1926.

Pignatelli, Jacobus, *Novissimae Consultationes Canonicae*, 2 vols. in 1, Cosmopoli, 1711.

Pirhing, Ernricus, *Jus Canonicum Nova Methodo Explicatum*, 5 vols. in 4, Dilingae, 1674-1678.

Potthast, Augustus, *Regesta Pontificum Romanorum inde ab anno post Christum natum MCXCVIII ad annum MCCCIV*, 2 vols., Berolini, 1874-1875.

Purcell, John B., *The Vickers and Purcell Controversy*, 2. ed., Cincinnati: Benziger Bros., 1868.

Reiffenstuel, Anacletus, *Jus Canonicum Universum*, 5 vols. in 7, Parisiis, 1864-1870.

Ryan, Gerald Aloysius, *Principles of Episcopal Jurisdiction*, The Catholic University of America Canon Law Studies, n. 120, Washington, D. C.: The Catholic University of America Press, 1939.

Schmalzgrueber, Franciscus, *Jus Ecclesiasticum Universum*, 5 vols. in 12, Romae, 1843-1845.

Slosser, Gaius Jackson, *Christian Unity, Its History and Challenge*, London: Kegan Paul, Trench, Trubner & Co., Ltd., 1929.

Steinbacher, Nicholas-Berg, Joseph Frederick, *Discussion held in Lebanon, Pa., on Mon., Tues., Wed., 17, 18, 19 Oct., 1842, between Nicholas Steinbacher of the Roman Catholic and Joseph Frederick Berg of the Reformed Church*, Philadelphia, 1842.

Suarez, Franciscus, *Opera Omnia*, ed. nova, a Carolo Berton, 26 vols., Parisiis, apud Ludovicum Vives, 1856-1866.

Thomas Aquinas, St., *Summa Theologica*, Taurini: Marietti, 1932.

Thureau-Dangin, Paul, *The English Catholic Revival in the Nineteenth Century*, revised and re-edited from a translation by the late Wilfred Wilberforce, 2 vols., London: Simpkin, Marshall, Hamilton, Kent & Co., Ltd., 1914.

Tris, A. C., *Search Light, The Testimony of the Bible Versus the Parliament of Religions*, Des Moines: Iowa Printing Co., 1893.

Vacant, E., Mangenot, E., et Amann, A., *Dictionnaire de Theologie Catholique*, Paris, 1908—

Vermeersch, Arthurus, *Theologiae Moralis Principia-Responsa-Consilia*, 3. ed., 4. vols., Romae: Universitá Gregoriana, 1933.

Vermeersch, Arthurus-Creusen, J., *Epitome Iuris Canonici,* 3 vols., Mechliniae-Romae: H. Dessain, Vol. I, 5. ed., 1934; Vol. II, 5. ed., 1936; Vol. III, 6. ed., 1937.

Ward, Wilfred, *The Life and Times of Cardinal Wiseman,* 2. ed., 2 vols., London: Longmans, Green & Co., 1897.

Wernz, Franciscus-Vidal, Petrus, *Ius Canonicum ad Codicis Normam Exactum,* 7 vols. in 8, Romae: apud Aedes Universitatis Gregorianae, 1923-1938.

PERIODICALS

Analecta Ecclesiastica, Romae, 1893-1911.

Ecclesiastical Review, The (originally *The American Ecclesiastical Review*), Philadelphia, 1889—

Etudes, Paris, 1856—

Periodica de Re Canonica et Morali utili Praesertim Religiosis et Missionariis, Brugis, 1905—

Theological Studies, Baltimore, 1939—

PRINCIPAL ARTICLES

Bouscaren, T. Lincoln, "Cooperation with Non-Catholics, Canonical Legislation"—*Theological Studies,* III (1942), 475-512.

Connell, Francis J., "Catholics and 'Interfaith' Groups"—*The Ecclesiastical Review,* CV (1941), 337-353.

Dudon, Paul, "La Conférence Chrétienne de Stockholm"—*Etudes,* CLXXXV (1925), 641-657.

Loiselet, Victor, "Ce que pense l'Église des conférences contradictoires"—*Etudes,* CIV (1905), 480-492.

ABBREVIATIONS

AAS—Acta Apostolicae Sedis.

C—Codex (Justinianus).

C. Th.—*Codex Theodosianus.*

Fontes—Codicis Iuris Canonici Fontes cura—Gasparri editi.

J. L.—*Regesta Pontificum Romanorum ab condita Ecclesia ad annum post Christum natum MCXCVIII.*

Mansi—*Sacrorum Conciliorum Nova et Amplissima Collectio.*

*MPG—*Migne, *Patrologia Graeca.*

*MPL—*Migne, *Patrologia Latina.*

Periodica—Periodica de Re Canonica et Morali utili Praesertim Religiosis et Missionariis.

Potthast—*Regesta Pontificum Romanorum inde ab anno post Christum natum MCXCVIII ad annum MCCCIV.*

ALPHABETICAL INDEX

BIOGRAPHICAL NOTE

Stephen Joseph Kelleher was born in New York City on August 31, 1915. He received his primary education at St. Jerome's parochial school, New York City. After one year at St. Agnes High School, he completed his high school and college studies in St. Joseph's Seminary and College, New York and Yonkers, from which institution he received the degree of Bachelor of Arts in 1936. In October, 1936, he was appointed to the North American College, Rome, Italy, to make his theological studies at the Pontifical Gregorian University, where he received the Baccalaureate in Theology in 1938. He made the last year of his theological studies at St. Joseph's Seminary, Yonkers, and was ordained to the priesthood on May 18, 1940. In September, 1940, he entered the Canon Law School at the Catholic University of America, Washington, D. C., where he received the Baccalaureate in Canon Law in June, 1941, and the Licentiate in Canon Law in the same month of the following year.

CANON LAW STUDIES *

1. FRERIKS, REV. CELESTINE A., C.PP.S., J.C.D., Religious Congregations in Their External Relations, 121 pp., 1916.
2. GALLIHER, REV. DANIEL M., O.P., J.C.D., Canonical Elections, 117 pp., 1917.
3. BORKOWSKI, REV. AURELIUS L., O.F.M., J.C.D., De Confraternitatibus Ecclesiasticis, 136 pp., 1918.
4. CASTILLO, REV. CAYO, J.C.D., Disertacion Historico-Canonica sobre la Potestad del Cabildo en Sede Vacante o Impedida del Vicario Capitular, 99 pp., 1919 (1918).
5. KUBELBECK, REV. WILLIAM J., S.T.B., J.C.D., The Sacred Penitentiaria and Its Relation to Faculties of Ordinaries and Priests, 129 pp., 1918.
6. PETROVITS, REV. JOSEPH, J.C., S.T.D., J.C.D., The New Church Law on Matrimony, X-461 pp., 1919.
7. HICKEY, REV. JOHN J., S.T.B., J.C.D., Irregularities and Simple Impediments in the New Code of Canon Law, 100 pp., 1920.
8. KLEKOTKA, REV. PETER J., S.T.B., J.C.D., Diocesan Consultors, 179 pp., 1920.
9. WANENMACHER, REV. FRANCIS, J.C.D., The Evidence in Ecclesiastical Procedure Affecting the Marriage Bond, 1920 (Printed 1935).
10. GOLDEN, REV. HENRY FRANCIS, J.C.D., Parochial Benefices in the New Code, IV-119 pp., 1921 (Printed 1925).
11. KOUDELKA, REV. CHARLES J., J.C.D., Pastors, Their Rights and Duties According to the New Code of Canon Law, 211 pp., 1921.
12. MELO, REV. ANTONIUS, O.F.M., J.C.D., De Exemptione Regularium, X-188 pp., 1921.
13 SCHAAF, REV. VALENTINE THEODORE, O.F.M., S.T.B., J.C.D., The Cloister, X-180 pp., 1921.
14. BURKE, REV. THOMAS JOSEPH, S.T.D., J.C.D., Competence in Ecclesiastical Tribunals, IV-117 pp., 1922.
15. LEECH, REV. GEORGE LEO, J.C.D., A Comparative Study of the Constitution "Apostolicae Sedis" and the "Codex Juris Canonici," 179 pp., 1922.
16. MOTRY, REV. HUBERT LOUIS, S.T.D., J.C.D., Diocesan Faculties According to the Code of Canon Law, II-167 pp., 1922.
17. MURPHY, REV. GEORGE LAWRENCE, J.C.D., Delinquencies and Penalties in the Administration and the Reception of the Sacraments, IV-121 pp., 1923.
18. O'REILLY, REV. JOHN ANTHONY, S.T.B., J.C.D., Ecclesiastical Sepulture in the New Code of Canon Law, II-129 pp., 1923.

---

* Below n. 100 only the following numbers are still available: Nn. 3, 4, 9, 25, 34, 57 and 75. Beginning with n. 100 only the following are unavailable: Nn. 100, 101, 102, 104, 105, 107, 108, 109, 111 and 113.

19. MICHALICKA, REV. WENCESLAS CYRILL, O.S.B., J.C.D., Judicial Procedure in Dismissal of Clerical Exempt Religious, 107 pp., 1923.

20. DARGIN, REV. EDWARD VINCENT, S.T.B., J.C.D., Reserved Cases According to the Code of Canon Law, IV-103 pp., 1924.

21. GODFREY, REV. JOHN A., S.T.B., J.C.D., The Right of Patronage According to the Code of Canon Law, 153 pp., 1924.

22. HAGEDORN, REV. FRANCIS EDWARD, J.C.D., General Legislation on Indulgences, II-154 pp., 1924.

23. KING, REV. JAMES IGNATIUS, J.C.D., The Administration of the Sacraments to Dying Non-Catholics, V-141 pp., 1924.

24. WINSLOW, REV. FRANCIS JOSEPH, O.F.M., J.C.D., Vicars and Prefects Apostolic, IV-149 pp., 1924.

25. CORREA, REV. JOSE SERVELION, S.T.L., J.C.D., La Potestad Legislativa de la Iglesia Catolica, IV-127 pp., 1925.

26. DUGAN, REV. HENRY FRANCIS, A.M., J.C.D., The Judiciary Department of the Diocesan Curia, 87 pp., 1925.

27. KELLER, REV. CHARLES FREDERICK, S.T.B., J.C.D., Mass Stipends, 167 pp., 1925.

28. PASCHANG, REV. JOHN LINUS, J.C.D., The Sacramentals According to the Code of Canon Law, 129 pp., 1925.

29. PIONTEK, REV. CYRILLUS, O.F.M., S.T.B., J.C.D., De Indulto Exclaustrationis necnon Saecularizationis, XIII-289 pp., 1925.

30. KEARNEY, REV. RICHARD JOSEPH, S.T.B., J.C.D., Sponsors at Baptism According to the Code of Canon Law, IV-127 pp., 1925.

31. BARTLETT, REV. CHESTER JOSEPH, A.M., LL.B., J.C.D., The Tenure of Parochial Property in the United States of America, V-108 pp., 1926.

32. KILKER, REV. ADRIAN JEROME, J.C.D., Extreme Unction, V-425 pp., 1926.

33. McCORMICK, REV. ROBERT EMMETT, J.C.D., Confessors of Religious, VIII-266 pp., 1926.

34. MILLER, REV. NEWTON THOMAS, J.C.D., Founded Masses According to the Code of Canon Law, VII-93 pp., 1926.

35. ROELKER, REV. EDWARD G., S.T.D., J.C.D., Principles of Privilege According to the Code of Canon Law, XI-166 pp., 1926.

36. BAKALARCZYK, REV. RICHARDUS, M.I.C., J.U.D., De Novitiatu, VIII-208 pp., 1927.

37. PIZZUTI, REV. LAWRENCE, O.F.M., J.U.L., De Parochis Religiosis, 1927. (Not Printed.)

38. BLILEY, REV. NICHOLAS MARTIN, O.S.B., J.C.D., Altars According to the Code of Canon Law, XIX-132 pp., 1927.

39. BROWN, MR. BRENDAN FRANCIS, A.B., LL.M., J.U.D., The Canonical Juristic Personality with Special Reference to its Status in the United States of America, V-212 pp., 1927.

40. CAVANAUGH, REV. WILLIAM THOMAS, C.P., J.U.D., The Reservation of the Blessed Sacrament, VIII-101 pp., 1927.

41. DOHENY, REV. WILLIAM J., C.S.C., A.B., J.U.D., Church Property: Modes of Acquisition, X-118 pp., 1927.

42. FELDHAUS, REV. ALOYSIUS H., C.PP.S., J.C.D., Oratories, IX-141 pp., 1927.

43. KELLY, REV. JAMES PATRICK, A.B., J.C.D., The Jurisdiction of the Simple Confessor, X-208 pp., 1927.

44. NEUBERGER, REV. NICHOLAS J., J.C.D., Canon 6 or the Relation of the Codex Juris Canonici to the Preceding Legislation, V-95 pp., 1927.

45. O'KEEFE, REV. GERALD MICHAEL, J.C.D., Matrimonial Dispensations, Powers of Bishops, Priests, and Confessors, VIII-232 pp., 1927.

46. QUIGLEY, REV. JOSEPH A. M., A.B., J.C.D., Condemned Societies, 139 pp., 1927.

47. ZAPLOTNIK, REV. JOHANNES LEO, J.C.D., De Vicariis Foraneis, X-142 pp., 1927.

48. DUSKIE, REV. JOHN ALOYSIUS, A.B., J.C.D., The Canonical Status of the Orientals in the United States, VIII-196 pp., 1928.

49. HYLAND, REV. FRANCIS EDWARD, J.C.D., Excommunication, Its Nature, Historical Development and Effects, VIII-181 pp., 1928.

50. REINMANN, REV. GERALD JOSEPH, O.M.C., J.C.D., The Third Order Secular of Saint Francis, 201 pp., 1928.

51. SCHENK, REV. FRANCIS J., J.C.D., The Matrimonial Impediments of Mixed Religion and Disparity of Cult, XVI-318 pp., 1929.

52. COADY, REV. JOHN JOSEPH, S.T.D., J.U.D., A.M., The Appointment of Pastors, VIII-150 pp., 1929.

53. KAY, REV. THOMAS HENRY, J.C.D., Competence in Matrimonial Procedure, VIII-164 pp., 1929.

54. TURNER, REV. SIDNEY JOSEPH, C.P., J.U.D., The Vow of Poverty, XLIX-217 pp., 1929.

55. KEARNEY, REV. RAYMOND A., A.B., S.T.D., J.C.D., The Principles of Delegation, VII-149 pp., 1929.

56. CONRAN, REV. EDWARD JAMES, A.B., J.C.D., The Interdict,, V-163 pp., 1930.

57. O'NEILL, REV. WILLIAM H., J.C.D., Papal Rescripts of Favor, VII-218 pp., 1930.

58. BASTNAGEL, REV. CLEMENT VINCENT, J.U.D., The Appointment of Parochial Adjutants and Assistants, XV-257 pp., 1930.

59. FERRY, REV. WILLIAM A., A.B., J.C.D., Stole Fees, V-136 pp., 1930.

60. COSTELLO, REV. JOHN MICHAEL, A.B., J.C.D., Domicile and Quasi-Domicile, VII-201 pp., 1930.

61. KREMER, REV. MICHAEL NICHOLAS, A.B., S.T.B., J.C.D., Church Support in the United States, VI-136 pp., 1930.

62. ANGULO, REV. LUIS, C.M., J.C.D., Legislation de la Iglesia sobre la intencion en la application de la Santa Misa, VII-104 pp., 1931.

63. FREY, REV. WOLFGANG NORBERT, O.S.B., A.B., J.C.D., The Act of Religious Profession, VIII-174 pp., 1931.

64. ROBERTS, REV. JAMES BRENDAN, A.B., J.C.D., The Banns of Marriage, XIV-140 pp., 1931.

65. RYDER, REV. RAYMOND ALOYSIUS, A.B., J.C.D., Simony, IX-151 pp., 1931.

66. CAMPAGNA, REV. ANGELO, PH.D., J.U.D., Il Vicario Generale del Vescovo, VII-205 pp., 1931.

67. COX, REV. JOSEPH GODFREY, A.B., J.C.D., The Administration of Seminaries, VI-124 pp., 1931.

68. GREGORY, REV. DONALD J., J.U.D., The Pauline Privilege, XV-165 pp., 1931.

69. DONOHUE, REV. JOHN F., J.C.D., The Impediment of Crime, VII-110 pp., 1931.

70. DOOLEY, REV. EUGENE A., O.M.I., J.C.D., Church Law on Sacred Relics, IX-143 pp., 1931.

71. ORTH, REV. CLEMENT RAYMOND, O.M.C., J.C.D., The Approbation of Religious Institutes, 171 pp., 1931.

72. PERNICONE, REV. JOSEPH M., A.B., J.C.D., The Ecclesiastical Prohibition of Books, XII-267 pp., 1932.

73. CLINTON, REV. CONNELL, A.B., J.C.D., The Paschal Precept, IX-108 pp., 1932.

74. DONNELLY, REV. FRANCIS B., A.M., S.T.L., J.C.D., The Diocesan Synod, VIII-125 pp., 1932.

75. TORRENTE, REV. CAMILO, C.M.F., J.C.D., Las Processiones Sagradas, V-145 pp., 1932.

76. MURPHY, REV. EDWIN J., C.PP.S., J.C.D., Suspension Ex Informata Conscientia, XI-122 pp., 1932.

77. MacKENZIE, REV. ERIC F., A.M., S.T.L., J.C.D., The Delict of Heresy in its Commission, Penalization, Absolution, VII-124 pp., 1932.

78. LYONS, REV. AVITUS E., S.T.B., J.C.D., The Collegiate Tribunal of First Instance, XI-147 pp., 1932.

79. CONNOLLY, REV. THOMAS A., J.C.D., Appeals, XI-195 pp., 1932.

80. SANGMEISTER, REV. JOSEPH V., A.B., J.C.D., Force and Fear as Precluding Matrimonial Consent, V-211 pp., 1932.

81. JAEGER, REV. LEO A., A.B., J.C.D., The Administration of Vacant and Quasi-Vacant Episcopal Sees in the United States, IX-229 pp., 1932.

82. RIMLINGER, REV. HERBERT T., J.C.D., Error Invalidating Matrimonial Consent, VII-79 pp., 1932.

83. BARRETT, REV. JOHN D. M., S.S., J.C.D., A Comparative Study of the Third Plenary Council of Baltimore and the Code, IX-221 pp., 1932.

84. CARBERRY, REV. JOHN J., PH.D., S.T.D., J.C.D., The Juridical Form of Marriage, X-177 pp., 1934.

85. DOLAN, REV. JOHN L., A.B., J.C.D., The Defensor Vinculi, XII-157 pp., 1934.

86. HANNAN, REV. JEROME D., A.M., S.T.D., LL.B., J.C.D., The Canon Law of Wills, IX-517 pp., 1934.

87. LEMIEUX, REV. DELISE A., A.M., J.C.D., The Sentence in Ecclesiastical Procedure, IX-131 pp., 1934.

88. O'ROURKE, REV. JAMES J., A.B., J.C.D., Parish Registers, VII-109 pp., 1934.

89. TIMLIN, REV. BARTHOLOMEW, O.F.M., A.M., J.C.D., Conditional Matrimonial Consent, X-381 pp., 1934.

90. WAHL, REV. FRANCIS X., A.B., J.C.D., The Matrimonial Impediments of Consanguinity and Affinity, VI-125 pp., 1934.

91. WHITE, REV. ROBERT J., A.B., LL.B., S.T.B., J.C.D., Canonical Ante-Nuptial Promises and the Civil Law, VI-152 pp., 1934.

92. HERRERA, REV. ANTONIO PARRA, O.C.D., J.C.D., Legislacion Ecclesiastica sobra el Ayuno y la Abstinencia, XI-191 pp., 1935.

93. KENNEDY, REV. EDWIN J., J.C.D., The Special Matrimonial Process in Cases of Evident Nullity, X-165 pp., 1935.

94. MANNING, REV. JOHN J., A.B., J.C.D., Presumption of Law in Matrimonial Procedure, XI-111 pp., 1935.

95. MOEDER, REV. JOHN M., J.C.D., The Proper Bishop for Ordination and Dimissorial Letters, VII-135 pp., 1935.

96. O'MARA, REV. WILLIAM A., A.B., J.C.D., Canonical Causes for Matrimonial Dispensations, IX-155 pp., 1935.

97. REILLY, REV. PETER, J.C.D., Residence of Pastors, IX-81 pp., 1935.

98. SMITH, REV. MARINER T., O.P., S.T.Lr., J.C.D., The Penal Law for Religious, VIII-169 pp., 1935.

99. WHALEN, REV. DONALD W., A.M., J.C.D., The Value of Testimonial Evidence in Matrimonial Procedure, XIII-297 pp., 1935.

100. CLEARY, REV. JOSEPH F., J.C.D., Canonical Limitations on the Alienation of Church Property, VIII-141 pp., 1936.

101. GLYNN, REV. JOHN C., J.C.D., The Promoter of Justice, XX-337 pp., 1936.

102. BRENNAN, REV. JAMES H., S.S., M.A., S.T.B., J.C.D., The Simple Convalidation of Marriage, VI-135 pp., 1937.

103. BRUNINI, REV. JOSEPH BERNARD, J.C.D., The Clerical Obligations of Canons 139 and 142, X-121 pp., 137.

104. CONNOR, REV. MAURICE, A.B., J.C.D., The Administrative Removal of Pastors, VIII-159 pp., 1937.

105. GUILFOYLE, REV. MERLIN JOSEPH, J.C.D., Custom, XI-144 pp., 1937.

106. HUGHES, REV. JAMES AUSTIN, A.B., A.M., J.C.D., Witnesses in Criminal Trials of Clerics, IX-140 pp., 1937.

107. JANSEN, REV. RAYMOND J., A.B., S.T.L., J.C.D., Canonical Provisions for Catechetical Instruction, VII-153 pp., 1937.

108. KEALY, REV. JOHN JAMES, A.B., J.C.D., The Introductory Libellus in Church Court Procedure, XI-121 pp., 1937.

109. McMANUS, REV. JAMES EDWARD, C.SS.R., J.C.D., The Administration of Temporal Goods in Religious Institutes, XVI-196 pp., 1937.

110. MORIARTY, REV. EUGENE JAMES, J.C.D., Oaths in Ecclesiastical Courts, X-115 pp., 1937.
111. RAINIER, REV. ELIGIUS GEORGE, C.SS.R., J.C.D., Suspension of Clerics, XVII-249 pp., 1937.
112. REILLY, REV. THOMAS F., C.SS.R., J.C.D., Visitation of Religious, VI-195 pp., 1938.
113. MORIARTY, REV. FRANCIS E., C.SS.R., J.C.D., The Extraordinary Absolution from Censures, XV-334 pp., 1938.
114. CONNOLLY, REV. NICHOLAS P., J.C.D., The Canonical Erection of Parishes, X-132 pp., 1938.
115. DONOVAN, REV. JAMES JOSEPH, J.C.D., The Pastor's Obligation in Prenuptial Investigation, XII-322 pp., 1938.
116. HARRIGAN, REV. ROBERT J., M.A., S.T.B., J.C.D., The Radical Sanation of Invalid Marriages, VIII-208 pp., 1938.
117. BOFFA, REV. CONRAD HUMBERT, J.C.D., Canonical Provisions for Catholic Schools, VII-211 pp., 1939.
118. PARSONS, REV. ANSCAR JOHN, O.M.Cap., J.C.D., Canonical Elections, XII-236 pp., 1939.
119. REILLY, REV. EDWARD MICHAEL, A.B., J.C.D., The General Norms of Dispensation, XII-156 pp., 1939.
120. RYAN, REV. GERALD ALOYSIUS, A.B., J.C.D., Principles of Episcopal Jurisdiction, XII-172 pp., 1939.
121. BURTON, REV. FRANCIS JAMES, C.S.C., A.B., J.C.D., A Commentary on Canon 1125, X-222 pp., 1940.
122. MIASKIEWICZ, REV. FRANCIS SIGISMUND, J.C.D., Supplied Jurisdiction According to Canon 209, XII-340 pp., 1940.
123. RICE, REV. PATRICK WILLIAM, A.B., J.C.D., Proof of Death in Prenuptial Investigation, VIII-156 pp., 1940.
124. ANGLIN, REV. THOMAS FRANCIS, M.S., J.C.D., The Eucharistic Fast, VIII-183 pp., 1941.
125. COLEMAN, REV. JOHN JEROME, J.C.D., The Minister of Confirmation, VI-153 pp., 1941.
126. DOWNS, REV. JOSEPH EMMANUEL, A.B., J.C.D., The Concept of Clerical Immunity, XI-163 pp., 1941.
127. ESSWEIN, REV. ANTHONY ALBERT, J.C.D., Extrajudicial Penal Powers of Ecclesiastical Superiors, X-144 pp., 1941.
128. FARRELL, REV. BENJAMIN FRANCIS, M.A., S.T.L., J.C.D., The Rights and Duties of the Local Ordinary Regarding Congregations of Women Religious of Pontifical Approval, V-195 pp., 1941.
129. FEENEY, REV. THOMAS JOHN, A.B., S.T.L., J.C.D., Restitutio in Integrum, VI-169 pp., 1941.
130. FINDLAY, REV. STEPHEN WILLIAM, O.S.B., A.B., J.C.D., Canonical Norms Governing the Deposition and Degradation of Clerics, XVII-279 pp., 1941.

131. GOODWINE, REV. JOHN, A.B., S.T.L., J.C.D., The Right of the Church to Acquire Property, VIII-119 pp., 1941.

132. HESTON, REV. EDWARD LOUIS, C.S.C., Ph.D., S.T.D., J.C.D., The Alienation of Church Property in the United States, XII-222 pp., 1941.

133. HOGAN, REV. JAMES JOHN, A.B., S.T.L., J.C.D., Judicial Advocates and Procurators, XIII-200 pp., 1941.

134. KEALY, REV. THOMAS M., A.B., Litt.B., J.C.D., Dowry of Women Religious, IX-152 pp., 1941.

135. KEENE, REV. MICHAEL JAMES, O.S.B., J.C.D., Religious Ordinaries and Canon 198, V-164 pp., 1942.

136. KERIN, REV. CHARLES A., S.S., M.A., S.T.B., J.C.D., The Privation of Christian Burial, XVI-279 pp., 1941.

137. LOUIS, REV. WILLIAM FRANCIS, M.A., J.C.D., Diocesan Archives, X-101 pp., 1941.

138. McDEVITT, REV. GILBERT JOSEPH, A.B., J.C.D., Legitimacy and Legitimation, X-247 pp., 1941.

139. McDONOUGH, REV. THOMAS JOSEPH, A.B., J.C.D., Apostolic Administrators, X-217 pp., 1941.

140. MEIER, REV. CARL ANTHONY, A.B., J.C.D., Penal Administration Procedure Against Negligent Pastors, XI-240 pp., 1941.

141. SCHMIDT, REV. JOHN ROGG, A.B., J.C.D., The Principles of Authentic Interpretation in Canon 17 of the Code of Canon Law, XII-331 pp., 1941.

142. SLAFKOSKY, REV. ANDREW LEONARD, A.B., J.C.D., The Canonical Episcopal Visitation of the Diocese, X-197 pp., 1941.

143. SWOBODA, REV. INNOCENT ROBERT, O.F.M., J.C.D., Ignorance in Relation to the Imputability of Delicts, IX-271 pp., 1941.

144. DUBÉ, REV. ARTHUR JOSEPH, A.B., J.C.D., The General Principles for the Reckoning of Time in Canon Law, VIII-299 pp., 1941.

145. McBRIDE, REV. JAMES T., A.B., J.C.D., Incardination and Excardination of Seculars, XX-585 pp., 1941.

146. KRÓL, REV. JOHN T., J.C.D., The Defendant in Ecclesiastical Trials, XII-207 pp., 1942.

147. COMYNS, REV. JOSEPH J., C.SS.R., A.B., J.C.D., Papal and Episcopal Administration of Church Property, XIV-155 pp., 1942.

148. BARRY, REV. GARRETT FRANCIS, O.M.I., J.C.D., Violation of the Cloister, XII-260 pp., 1942.

149. BOLDUC, REV. GATIEN, C.S.V., A.B., S.T.L., J.C.D., Les Études dans les Religions Cléricales, VIII-155 pp., 1942.

150. BOYLE, REV. DAVID JOHN, M.A., J.C.D., The Juridic Effects of Moral Certitude on Pre-Nuptial Guarantees, XII-188 pp., 1942.

151. CANAVAN, REV. WALTER JOSEPH, M.A., LITT.D., J.C.D., The Profession of Faith, XII-143 pp., 1942.

152. DESROCHERS, REV. BRUNO, A.B., PH.L., S.T.B., J.C.D., Le Premier Concile Plénier de Québec et le Code de Droit Canonique, XIV-186 pp., 1942.

153. DILLON, REV. ROBERT EDWARD, A.B., J.C.D., Common Law Marriage, X-148 pp., 1942.

154. DODWELL, REV. EDWARD JOHN, PH.D., S.T.B., J.C.L., The Time and Place for the Celebration of Marriage.

155. DONNELLAN, REV. THOMAS ANDREW, A.B., J.C.D., The Obligation of the Missa pro Populo, VII-131 pp., 1942.

156. ELTZ, REV. LOUIS ANTHONY, A.B., J.C.L., Cooperation in Crime.

157. GASS, REV. SYLVESTER FRANCIS, M.A., J.C.D., Ecclesiastical Pensions, XI-206 pp., 1942.

158. GUINIVEN, REV. JOHN JOSEPH, C.SS.R., J.C.D., The Precept of Hearing Mass, XIV-188 pp., 1942.

159. GULCZYNSKI, REV. JOHN THEOPHILUS, J.C.L., The Desecration and Violation of Churches.

160. HAMMILL, REV. JOHN LEO, M.A., J.C.D., The Obligations of the Traveler According to Canon 14, VIII-204 pp., 1942.

161. HAYDT, REV. JOHN JOSEPH, A.B., J.C.D., Reserved Benefices, XI-148 pp., 1942.

162. HUSER, REV. ROGER JOHN, O.F.M., A.B., J.C.L., The Crime of Abortion in Canon Law.

163. KEARNEY, REV. FRANCIS PATRICK, A.B., S.T.L., J.C.L., The Principles of Canon 1127.

164. LINAHEN, REV. LEO JAMES, S.T.L., J.C.D., De Absolutione Complicis In Peccato Turpi, 114 pp., 1942.

165. MCCLOSKEY, REV. JOSEPH ALOYSIUS, A.B., J.C.D., The Subject of Ecclesiastical Law According to Canon 12, XVII-246 pp., 1942.

166. O'NEILL, REV. FRANCIS JOSEPH, C.SS.R., J.C.D., The Dismissal of Religious in Temporary Vows, XIII-220 pp., 1942.

167. PRINCE, REV. JOHN EDWARD, A.B., S.T.B., J.C.D., The Diocesan Chancellor, X-136 pp., 1942.

168. RIESNER, REV. ALBERT JOSEPH, C.SS.R., J.C.D., Apostates and Fugitives from Religious Institutes, IX-168 pp., 1942.

169. STENGER, REV. JOSEPH BERNARD, J.C.D., The Mortgaging of Church Property, 186 pp., 1942.

170. WALDRON, REV. JOSEPH FRANCIS, A.B., J.C.D., The Minister of Baptism, XII-197 pp., 1942.

171. WILLETT, REV. ROBERT ALBERT, J.C.D., The Probative Value of Documents in Ecclesiastical Trials, X-124 pp., 1942.

172. WOEBER, REV. EDWARD MARTIN, M.A., J.C.D., The Interpellations, XII-161 pp., 1942.

173. BENKO, REV. MATTHEW ALOYSIUS, O.S.B., M.A., J.C.L., The Abbot *Nullius*.

174. CHRIST, REV. JOSEPH JAMES, M.A., S.T.L., J.C.L., Dispensation from Vindicative Penalties.

175. CLANCY, REV. PATRICK M. J., O.P., A.B., S.T.LR., J.C.L., The Local Religious Superior.

176. CLARKE, REV. THOMAS JAMES, J.C.L., Parish Societies.

177. CONNOLLY, REV. JOHN PATRICK, S.T.L., J.C.L., Synodal Examiners and Parish Priest Consultors.

178. DRUMM, REV. WILLIAM MARTIN, A.B., J.C.L., Hospital Chaplains.

179. FLANAGAN, REV. BERNARD JOSEPH, A.B., S.T.L., J.C.L., The Canonical Erection of Religious Houses.

180. KELLEHER, REV. STEPHEN JOSEPH, A.B., S.T.B., J.C.L., Discussions with Non-Catholics: Canonical Legislation.

181. LEWIS, REV. GORDIAN, C.P., J.C.L., Chapters in Religious Institutes.

182. MARX, REV. ADOLPH, J.C.L., The Declaration of Nullity of Marriages Contracted Outside the Church.

183. MATULENAS, REV. RAYMOND ANTHONY, O.S.B., A.B., J.C.L., Communication, a Source of Privileges.

184. O'LEARY, REV. CHARLES GERARD, C.SS.R., Religious Dismissed After Perpetual Profession.

185. POWER, REV. CORNELIUS MICHAEL, J.C.L., The Blessing of Cemeteries.

186. SHUHLER, REV. RALPH VINCENT, O.S.A., J.C.L., Privileges of Religious to Absolve and Dispense.

187. ZIOLKOWSKI, REV. THADDEUS STANISLAUS, A.B., J.C.L., The Consecration and Blessing of Churches.

CPSIA information can be obtained
at www.ICGtesting.com
Printed in the USA
BVHW032131180119
538228BV00005B/135/P